GOD'S LOVE COMPELS US

Other Books by the Gospel Coalition

Don't Call It a Comeback: The Old Faith for a New Day, edited by Kevin DeYoung

Entrusted with the Gospel: Pastoral Expositions of 2 Timothy, edited by D. A. Carson

The Gospel as Center: Renewing Our Faith and Reforming Our Ministry Practices, edited by D. A. Carson and Timothy Keller

Here Is Our God: God's Revelation of Himself in Scripture, edited by Kathleen B. Nielson and D. A. Carson

His Mission: Jesus in the Gospel of Luke, edited by D. A. Carson and Kathleen B. Nielson

The Scriptures Testify about Me: Jesus and the Gospel in the Old Testament, edited by D. A. Carson

The Gospel Coalition Booklets
Edited by D. A. Carson and Timothy Keller

Baptism and the Lord's Supper, by Thabiti M. Anyabwile and J. Ligon Duncan

Can We Know the Truth?, by Richard D. Phillips

Christ's Redemption, by Sandy Willson

The Church: God's New People, by Timothy Savage

Creation, by Andrew M. Davis

The Gospel and Scripture: How to Read the Bible, by Mike Bullmore

Gospel-Centered Ministry, by D. A. Carson and Timothy Keller

The Holy Spirit, by Kevin L. DeYoung

Justification, by Philip Graham Ryken

The Kingdom of God, by Stephen T. Um

The Plan, by Colin S. Smith

The Restoration of All Things, by Sam Storms

Sin and the Fall, by Reddit Andrews III

What Is the Gospel?, by Bryan Chapell

GOD'S LOVE COMPELS US

TAKING THE GOSPEL TO THE WORLD

D. A. CARSON AND KATHLEEN B. NIELSON, EDITORS

CROSSWAY

WHEATON, ILLINOIS

Library of Congress Cataloging-in-Publication Data

    God's love compels us : taking the gospel to the world / D. A. Carson and Kathleen B. Nielson, editors.
        pages cm
    "The Gospel Coalition."
    Includes bibliographical references and index.
    ISBN 978-1-4335-4379-1 (tp)
    1. Missions—Congresses. 2. Bible. Corinthians, 2nd, IV, 1–V, XXI—Criticism, interpretation, etc.—Congresses. I. Carson, D. A., editor.
    BV2020.G63   2015
    266—dc23   2014034077

Crossway is a publishing ministry of Good News Publishers.

VP		25	24	23	22	21	20	19	18	17	16	15
15	14	13	12	11	10	9	8	7	6	5	4	3	2	1

CONTENTS

PREFACE

One of the most encouraging signs in recent years of God's hand of blessing has been the surprising number of serious students who are coming forward for theological training. Students often come through seminaries in distinguishable waves, and many of us who have been teachers for a few decades gladly testify that the current wave is one of the most encouraging we have seen. Thousands of young men want to be church planters, and they are looking for teachers and mentors who will spend time with them. Others, both men and women, simply want to handle Scripture better, to learn how to do evangelism and Bible studies in the transcultural environments of our big cities, or to write with clarity, faithfulness, humility, and unction. Neither is this phenomenon happening in America alone: in various degrees, in many countries, serious students are coming to grips with the serious nature of the gospel, and wanting to serve.

Some of the men on the Council of The Gospel Coalition, and a few others, began to wonder if some of this grace-driven energy should be challenged with the needs beyond America's borders. Even though world mission is no longer "from the West to the rest," but more like "from everywhere to everywhere," the worldwide needs are gigantic. Not only do thousands of unreached people groups remain, but there are far larger populations where knowledge of Scripture is desperately thin, where nominalism or syncretism reigns supreme, and where the gospel is poorly understood and widely disbelieved. So we decided that, ahead of the 2013 National Conference of the Coalition, we would sponsor a preconference on world mission, designed especially, though not exclusively, for students. That took place in April 2013. Before the year was out, the Cross Conference organized a further mission conference in Louisville—longer, more detailed, but with similar hopes and vision.

The chapters of this book are slightly edited print forms of the seven plenary addresses of the April 2013 mission conference. Four of them are devoted to exposition of 2 Corinthians 4–5. As usual, we encouraged a diversity of styles of exposition, provided that the Word of God was faithfully unpacked, so that people might better see the glory of God in the gospel. Also, because mission theology is today challenged by a handful of "hot topics," we decided to devote three plenaries to address some of them: Andrew Davis spoke on "Are People without Christ Really Lost?"; Michael Oh addressed "The Individual's Suffering and the Salvation of the World"; and Stephen Um spoke on "Jesus and Justice." Though they are topically arranged, all of these chapters are packed with thoughtful, substantial biblical reflection.

I am grateful beyond words to the plenary speakers for being willing to provide full manuscripts; to Kathleen Nielson for her careful administrative and editorial work; and to Crossway for continuing to make so much of the audio and video ministry of TGC available in print form.

Soli Deo gloria.

Don Carson
President, TGC

1

THE BIBLICAL BASIS FOR MISSIONS

Treasure in Jars of Clay

2 CORINTHIANS 4:1–12

D. A. Carson

What is the biblical basis for missions? And how shall we go about answering that question?

We might simply tease out the Bible's entire storyline. We begin with creation: God makes everything good. Then comes the anarchic revolution against God that Christians call "the fall." Yet, wonderfully, as early as Genesis 3:15, God himself promises that the seed of the woman will crush the Serpent's head. In perfect justice, God could destroy the race at that point, but already he is promising redemption. And then, a few chapters later, when hatred and idolatry multiply, he could wipe out the entire race in the flood, but he spares eight human beings.

As evil and idolatry multiply yet again, God starts, as it were, a new humanity, calling Abraham as the patriarch of a new race. From Abraham's seed, God avers, all the nations of the earth will be blessed. Yet Abraham, though he is called a friend of God and a man of faith, manages, more than once, to be a liar whose deceit puts his wife in jeopardy. His son appears to be a bit of a wimp. His grandson Jacob is a deceiver. Jacob's sons, the twelve patriarchs— well, one sleeps with his father's concubine and another messes around with his own daughter-in-law. Two of them butcher all the males of a small village, while ten of them try to decide whether to kill the eleventh or sell him into slavery. And these are the patriarchs! Even so, God spares them, preserving the promised line until, toward the end of the book of Genesis, there is a promise that from one of these patriarchs will eventually spring a redeeming king, the Lion of the tribe of Judah.

In the book of Exodus, God constitutes the Israelites a nation and gives them the law. This instruction commands certain behavior; it also institutes certain rites and rituals that anticipate what is yet to come. The sacrifices of the Day of Atonement, for example, offered up for the sins of the priest and of the people, repeated year after year, have the effect of reminding God's people of their sins even as they serve as the means by which God forgives them.

Soon we arrive at the utter degeneration described in the book of Judges—endless cycles of depravity, sinking lower and lower until, by the end of the period covered in the book, the scene is so dark that you cannot tell the good guys from the bad guys. Even the good guys are frankly so embarrassing and barbaric that the chapters describing them are difficult to read in public. "O God, how we need a king, for everyone is doing what is right in his own eyes."

Eventually, God raises up David, described as "a man after his own heart" (1 Sam. 13:14). This man after God's heart manages to commit adultery and murder. One wonders what he would have done if he hadn't been a man after God's heart. That dynasty rules over the twelve tribes for only two generations; then the nation splits. Two centuries later, wallowing in corruption, idolatry, depravity, endless malice, and greed, the ten northern tribes go into captivity. A century and a half after that, the southern tribes, passionately enjoying similar sins, experience the same judgment.

In this short chapter, I cannot flesh out Israel's further experiences, not to mention the diverse ways in which God speaks to them, displaying amazing patience. But we would be remiss to forget the words of some of the prophets. One of them foresees a coming servant who will be wounded for our transgressions (Isaiah 53). That same prophet also foresees a day when God will say, "In that day Israel will be the third, along with Egypt and Assyria, a blessing on the earth" (19:24),[1] anticipating a time when the locus of the people of God will not be one nation or one tribe: "The LORD Almighty will bless them saying, 'Blessed be Egypt my people, Assyria my handiwork, and Israel my inheritance'" (v. 25).

In the fullness of time, we come to the Lord Jesus, his ministry, his death and resurrection, and the Great Commission. Empowering his people to do what he commands, Christ bestows the Holy Spirit. The closing chapters of the Bible display a consummating vision of men and women, drawn from every tongue, tribe, people, and nation, one redeemed community, the blood-bought from around the world, gathered around the throne of God in resurrection splendor.

In other words, we could assert that the biblical basis for missions is nothing other than the storyline of the entire Bible: God graciously goes after sinners and wins over a vast number of them.

Alternatively, we might simply focus on Jesus himself. We could consider, for example, his various titles and functions. He is the King, and as the King, he declares: "All authority in heaven and on earth has been given to me. Therefore go and make disciples" (Matt. 28:18–19). Or we might reflect on the fact that Jesus is the Good Shepherd who gives his life for his sheep. Again, Jesus is the High Priest who offers himself as the perfect sacrifice. He is the Word of God—God's ultimate self-expression, declared to the entire world. Or we might meditate on the obedience of Christ. In Gethsemane, his prayer is not, "Oh, I really do want to go through with this because I really love those sinners so much"; rather, he

---

[1] Unless otherwise indicated, Scripture references in this chapter are from The Holy Bible, New International Version®, NIV®. Copyright © 1973, 1978, 1984, 2011 by Biblica, Inc.™ Used by permission. All rights reserved worldwide.

prays, "Not my will, but yours be done" (Luke 22:42). The driving power behind Jesus's determination to go to the cross is, first of all, his obedience to his Father. This is the heavenly Father's plan, and the world must know, Jesus says in John 14, that he always does what pleases his Father. Again, we might consider great events in Jesus's mission and their bearing on the biblical basis of missions: the cross, the resurrection, his session at the Father's right hand, or the second coming, when every knee shall bow to him. There are so many legitimate ways to establish the biblical basis of missions.

Yet another way of getting at the biblical basis for missions is to focus on a specific passage. There are many texts to which we could turn, but I will fasten our attention on 2 Corinthians 4:1–12:

Therefore, since through God's mercy we have this ministry, we do not lose heart. Rather, we have renounced secret and shameful ways; we do not use deception, nor do we distort the word of God. On the contrary, by setting forth the truth plainly we commend ourselves to everyone's conscience in the sight of God. And even if our gospel is veiled, it is veiled to those who are perishing. The god of this age has blinded the minds of unbelievers, so that they cannot see the light of the gospel that displays the glory of Christ, who is the image of God. For what we preach is not ourselves, but Jesus Christ as Lord, and ourselves as your servants for Jesus' sake. For God, who said, "Let light shine out of darkness," made his light shine in our hearts to give us the light of the knowledge of God's glory displayed in the face of Christ. But we have this treasure in jars of clay to show that this all-surpassing power is from God and not from us. We are hard pressed on every side, but not crushed; perplexed, but not in despair; persecuted, but not abandoned; struck down, but not destroyed. We always carry around in our body the death of Jesus, so that the life of Jesus may also be revealed in our body. For we who are alive are always being given over to death for Jesus' sake, so that his life may also be revealed in our mortal body. So then, death is at work in us, but life is at work in you.

How does this passage contribute to our grasp of the biblical basis for missions? Verse 1 opens by talking about this ministry we have: "Since through God's mercy we have this ministry, we do not lose heart." This ministry, according to verse 2, is bound up with setting forth the truth plainly. According to verse 4, we are placarding the light of the gospel that displays the glory of Christ, who is the image of God. When we discharge this ministry, we are nothing more than clay pots (according to v. 7 and following). And yet, all this achieves eternal glory (v. 17) as we fix our eyes on what is unseen (now, there's a paradox!)—unseen but eternal. These verses do not so much *define* world mission as *describe* it. Sometimes the most powerful and moving basis for world mission lies in the Bible's depiction of what it looks like.

It will be helpful, I think, to unpack three parts of this description.

1. Gospel Ministry Demands Unqualified Integrity (vv. 1–3)

In our English Bible, this passage begins with the word *therefore*. When I was a little whippersnapper, my father, who was trying to teach me elementary interpretation principles, said, "Don, whenever you see a *wherefore* or *therefore*, see what it's there for." In this case, *therefore* connects the previous chapter with what is found in our verses. Second Corinthians 3 establishes the fact that apostolic ministry, the ministry of Paul in particular, is blessed with many privileged advantages over the ministry of Moses at the time of the giving of the law. To put it another way, the ministry of the new covenant sealed in Jesus's blood is superior to the ministry of the old covenant. So we read in chapter 3:

> Such confidence we have through Christ before God. Not that we are competent in ourselves to claim anything for ourselves, but our competence comes from God. He has made us

competent as ministers of a new covenant—not of the letter but of the Spirit; for the letter kills, but the Spirit gives life. (vv. 4–6)

Again, note some of the contrasts between the two covenants as they're teased out later in chapter 3:

> Now if the ministry that brought death [that is, ministry under the law], which was engraved in letters on stone [referring to the Ten Commandments], came with glory, so that the Israelites could not look steadily at the face of Moses because of its glory, transitory though it was, will not the ministry of the Spirit be even more glorious? If the ministry that brought condemnation was glorious, how much more glorious is the ministry that brings righteousness! (vv. 7–9)

Again:

> And we all, who with unveiled faces contemplate the Lord's glory, are being transformed into his image with ever-increasing glory, which comes from the Lord, who is the Spirit. (v. 18)

Then comes chapter 4:

> Therefore, since through God's mercy we have this ministry, we do not lose heart. (v. 1)

In other words, Paul understands full well that Christian ministry, despite its deep privileges, coughs up many reasons for losing heart, many reasons for deep discouragement. But since it is through God's mercy that we have this ministry, and since, as 2 Corinthians 3 has shown, this ministry belongs to the surpassingly wonderful new covenant, *therefore,* we do not lose heart.

Before we go any further, we should ask two questions.

First, do these references to "this ministry" or "our ministry" refer only to apostolic ministry? If so, we should be cautious about applying them to us and to the work of world mission today. But although 2 Corinthians 3 focuses on Paul and apostolic ministry, at the end of chapter 3 and right through chapters 4 and 5, Paul elides the discussion into the ministry of all believers. You can see this, for example, at the end of chapter 3: "And *we all*, who with unveiled faces contemplate the Lord's glory, are being transformed into his image with ever-increasing glory, which comes from the Lord, who is the Spirit" (v. 18). Again, in chapter 5: "So we make it our goal to please him, whether we are at home in the body or away from it. For we must all appear before the judgment seat of Christ" (vv. 9–10a).

So although Paul begins with his own ministry (and, doubtless, that is in some ways a model for all of us in any case), he specifically elides the discussion into so broad a set of parameters that he includes Christians like you and me.

The second question: What is the nature of the discouragement that Paul faces? Why is he tempted to lose heart, granted all of these incredible privileges belonging to the new covenant? It is pretty obvious that many people are offended by the straight talk of Scripture. That is surely what hides behind verse 2:

> We have renounced secret and shameful ways; we do not use deception, nor do we distort the word of God. On the contrary, by setting forth the truth plainly we commend ourselves to everyone's conscience in the sight of God.

Why would anyone use deception? Why would you use slightly shady language or ambiguous categories? The reason is that all of us know full well that some of what the Bible says isn't going to be too popular. So it becomes a perennial temptation to use softer language, to avoid the Bible's sharp edges and unyielding but often unpopular truths.

In every culture, many people absorb and then reflect their surrounding values and priorities without much critical thought. For example, you could have deep discussions with devout Muslims in the context of Islamic culture, and they may understand what you are saying at the level of your sentences and paragraphs, but fail to grasp what the gospel is about. They don't see it. They understand it at some level, but they do not see it. Or you could have deep discussions with hedonists who simply cannot really see the transcendent value of the gospel: they are blind to it. The god of this world has blinded them (4:4). Also, some common values in Western culture are painfully antagonistic to the gospel. For example, some popular forms of tolerance are remarkably intolerant: if you proclaim an exclusive Jesus today, you are readily dismissed as a bigot.

So what are your options? Well, of course, we might adopt "shameful ways" that "distort the word of God" (4:2). After all, everyone has his or her own point of view. Maybe Jesus is not the only way; maybe there are other ways of getting to God after all. Maybe Peter was sincere but sadly mistaken when he said that "there is no other name under heaven given to mankind by which we must be saved" (Acts 4:12). Maybe Jesus was exaggerating a bit when he said: "I am the way and the truth and the life. No one comes to the Father except through me" (John 14:6). After all, those sound like narrow-minded, bigoted, intolerant statements, don't they? But as a result of these distortions, the god of this age, of this particular culture, blinds the eyes of countless people. Again, it is very difficult for many younger people in this culture to think of themselves as guilty. We are much more prone to think of ourselves as victims. But how do we come to grips with a Savior who dies for our sin if, at the end of the day, we don't think of ourselves as sinners? Maybe what we really need is a Savior to take us out of the muck of our misfortune. Certainly today there is a pretty hard-nosed skepticism about the existence of hell. But the person who talks most about hell in the Bible is Jesus himself. It is pretty hard to say nothing about hell and be faithful to Jesus.

In other words, sometimes, quite frankly, the truth itself is what is offensive. Jesus knew that in his own day, of course. Do you remember the remarkable passage in John 8:45? He says to some interlocutors, "Because I tell the truth, you do not believe me!" It would be bad enough if that sentence began with a concessive instead of a causal: "*Although* I tell the truth, you do not believe me." That would be tragic. But the word by which Jesus introduces his charge is a causal: "*Because* I tell the truth, you do not believe me."

So again, what are your options? Tell untruths in order to get people to believe? What then will people believe? Untruths.

It can be very discouraging to articulate the truth, to preach the truth, only to discover that many people, far from simply listening and then rejecting the truth, write you off as a narrow-minded bigot. That is truly disheartening. It is worth remembering that in the first three centuries of the Christian church, until the time of Constantine, the most common pagan criticism against Christianity was that it was too narrow, too exclusive. Sound familiar?

Some of us have responded to the call to cross-cultural ministry, and we may have been tempted to think of ourselves as fledgling heroes of the faith. We may have read our share of missionary biographies and imagined how we, too, might be used of God to preach the gospel with great power and fruitfulness, instrumental in seeing hundreds converted, maybe thousands. Then, when we actually get there, we discover how difficult and even dangerous some places can be. We like to hear the stories of preachers and missionaries who were privileged to see enormous fruitfulness, but then, there's always a Samuel Zwemer, who preached forty years in the Muslim world and saw eight converts—and five of them were killed. It's enough to make a person lose heart.

Even Paul is tempted to lose heart, but, he says, "since through God's mercy we have this ministry, we do not lose heart." Rather:

> We have renounced secret and shameful ways; we do not use deception, nor do we distort the word of God. On the contrary, by setting forth the truth plainly we commend ourselves to everyone's conscience in the sight of God. And even if our gospel is veiled, it is veiled to those who are perishing. (2 Cor. 4:2–3)

Elsewhere, Paul faces other temptations. He writes in 2:17:

Unlike so many, we do not peddle the word of God for profit. On the contrary, in Christ we speak before God with sincerity, as those sent from God.

It is possible to shape your message to increase the income. Paul faced this temptation and rejected it.

A very different temptation emerges in 11:20–21:

In fact, you even put up with anyone who enslaves you or exploits you or takes advantage of you or puts on airs or slaps you in the face. To my shame I admit that we were too weak for that!

In other words, some people look for Christian preachers and missionaries who are bullies. They somehow feel secure if a strong man is telling them where to step off. But how does that breed character, the humility of Christ, godliness, and maturity that trains up leaders? "I admit that I was too weak for that," the apostle Paul says, his pen dripping in sarcasm.

No, no. He has resolved not to use deception, not to distort the Word of God, and not to peddle the Word for money. He is not going to try to win popularity or increase his income by slanting the truth. On the contrary, by setting forth the truth plainly, he says, we Christians "commend ourselves to everyone's conscience in the sight of God" (4:2). What is required is courage, backbone, resolve. Our priority is submission to the Word of God. So if you want to know what biblical mission looks like, hear this: gospel ministry demands unqualified integrity.

2. The Gospel Itself Displays the Glory of Christ (vv. 4–6)

Our task is to herald the gospel even if some cannot see its light. Paul says:

The god of this age has blinded the minds of unbelievers, so that they cannot see the light of the gospel that displays the glory of Christ, who is the image of God. (4:4)

Quite some years ago, I knew a young woman at the University of Cambridge, a graduate student to whom I had given a copy of the book *Basic Christianity* by John Stott. She read it carefully enough that she looked up a lot of the biblical references that littered its pages. When I asked her some weeks later what she made of it, she said, "I've decided that Christianity is for good people like you and Carol [her Christian roommate], but it's not for me."

How on earth does an intelligent graduate student at Cambridge manage to read an author like Stott, who writes with great clarity and limpid prose, and think that the gospel is all about being "good people"? When I heard her words, this passage came to mind: "The god of this age has blinded the minds of unbelievers, so that they cannot see the light of the gospel that displays the glory of Christ." They cannot see it.

What exactly does this gospel display? "The glory of Christ, who is the image of God" (v. 4)—or again, as Paul puts it in verse 5: we preach "not ourselves, but Jesus Christ as Lord." The notion of Jesus as the image of God is bound up in Paul's thought with the incarnation. Do you want to know what God looks like, when, after all, no one can gaze on him and live? Study Jesus. He is the image of God. Similarly, the epistle to the Hebrews tells us that Jesus is "the radiance of God's glory" (1:3). That's a bit like saying he's the light of God's light, the shining of his shining. He's the exact imprint of who he is. He's not only the effulgence, the radiance of God's glory, but "the exact representation of his being" (1:3). He is the image of God.

The gospel is bound up in the first place with Jesus and who he is—not just Jesus as a cipher, but Jesus who is thus identified with God himself. Small wonder we proclaim Jesus Christ as Lord. Undoubtedly that title was his before the world began: he was the Son of God before he became a human being, the man Jesus. But the confession "Jesus Christ as Lord" is bound up with his vindication as the resurrected God-man. His sacrifice has been accepted. Although he emptied himself and became a nobody, dying the ignominious death of a condemned criminal, God highly exalted him and gave him the name that is above every name, that at the name of Jesus every knee must bow (Phil. 2:9–10). We preach Jesus Christ as Lord.

In other words, this confession is predicated on Jesus's death and resurrection, on his cross work. We are never to imagine that the word *Jesus* is a magical religious "abracadabra" word: mention the name *Jesus* and you'll get answers to your prayers. Rather, we preach God incarnate—Christ crucified, risen again, vindicated, and sovereign—so that all of God's authority (according to 1 Corinthians 15) is mediated through him, until every knee bows on the last day and the last enemy, death itself, is destroyed. That is what we preach.

It is always worth asking, "What is the gospel?" We have to remember, first of all, that the gospel is news. That is what it is: dramatically powerful news, very largely good news. What do you do with news? You announce it. It is news about Jesus—about who Jesus is and what he has done by God's own decree, especially in his cross, resurrection, and ascension, in order to redeem men and women for himself from every tribe, tongue, people, and nation, to constitute this new blood-bought community as his church, the assembly of the living God, until, in God's purposes, the entire creation is swallowed up in a new heaven and a new earth, the home of righteousness, and there is resurrection existence on the last day. That's the good news.

The good news is not belief. Faith is the proper result of the good news. The good news is not an exhortation to turn over a new leaf. Certainly repentance is required because of the good news, but we announce *what God has done in Christ Jesus*. That's why Paul places much emphasis in our new covenant ministry on announcing and preaching Jesus. What we preach is not ourselves, but Jesus Christ as Lord, and in consequence of this, we are "your servants for Jesus' sake" (2 Cor. 4:5). The transformation, the obedience of faith, the love to do the Word of God—all of this flows out of the gospel. These things are the inevitable result of the gospel as it takes hold of people's lives. But what we preach, what we announce, is news about Jesus.

So if we have come to see the light of the gospel, Paul tells us, it is because God has "made his light shine in our hearts to give us the light of the knowledge of God's glory displayed in the face of Christ" (v. 6). In other words, if we have come to see the truth, it is not because we are brighter, more insightful, or Western. It is because God has somehow illumined our hearts. He has made his light shine in our hearts to give us the light of the knowledge of his glory.

The language is evocative of creation: "God said, 'Let there be light,' and there was light" (Gen. 1:3). The darkness could not stop it. Similarly, when we now preach this gospel, every conversion is a result of God's speaking again and saying, in effect: "Let there be light! Let light shine out of the darkness!"—and the darkness cannot stop it. Here is sovereign regeneration. Otherwise, the darkness remains. Bright graduate students at Cambridge read Stott and still remain in the darkness until God says, "Let there be light!" Then there is light.

My confidence, therefore, in heralding the light of the gospel that displays the glory of Christ, in obedience to his command, as a fruit of the mercy we have received in this ministry, is not that everyone will be impressed by my articulation of the truth and become adoring Christians. Rather, my confidence is that, again and again, whether to many or to few, God will say, "Let there be light"—and blind men and women will see. His light will shine into more hearts to give them the light of the knowledge of God's glory displayed in the face of Christ. If you want to know what the biblical basis for missions looks like, hear this: the gospel displays the glory of Christ.

3. Gospel Ministry Is Characterized by Paradoxical Death to Self and Overflowing Life in Christ (vv. 7–12)

I have a son. When he was a lad of about fifteen or sixteen, although his serious instruments were violin and viola, he was one of those chaps who could pick up almost any instrument and pretty shortly could get some decent sounds out of it. Somewhere along the line, he picked up an Irish penny whistle, and he became pretty good at it. One day he said to me: "Dad, you know what would be nice? If you made me a box for this." He knew, of course, that I dabble a bit in woodwork. I said: "Nicholas, that's a seven-dollar instrument. If I made a decent box, it would be worth ten times that amount, maybe more. If you lose this instrument or it goes rusty or something, buy another one. Buy ten! They're cheap." He said, "Yeah, Dad, but it'd be cool." Well, how could I possibly resist that? So I bought a nice piece of walnut, my favorite wood to work with, and shaped it and routed it out in the inside. I put in a velvet lining for the instrument, and shaped the wood to receive inlaid magnets, a piano hinge on the back, and, on the top, an inlaid brass plaque with his name, "Nicholas J. Carson." I buffed up that box and put a nice sheen on it. When I gave it to him, I told him it was his anti-gospel box. He said, "What do you mean?" I said: "Well, according to 2 Corinthians 4, with respect to the gospel, all the treasure is on the inside and on the outside is the cheap clay pot. This is the reverse."

But some of us act, now and then, as if all of the potency for the music of the gospel comes from the box. Paul won't have it:

> But we have this treasure [Christ and the gospel] in jars of clay to show that this all-surpassing power [the power that actually transforms people] is from God and not from us. We are hard pressed on every side, but not crushed; perplexed, but not in despair; persecuted, but not abandoned; struck down, but not destroyed. (2 Cor. 4:7–9)

If you have read on in 2 Corinthians to chapter 11, you know that Paul reminds you of some of the things that he has suffered for the sake of the gospel. By the time of his writing of this letter, he has been shipwrecked three times—and that's before the shipwreck recounted in Acts 27. Once, he spent a day and a night on the open sea. Five times he received the synagogue whipping—thirty-nine blows—and three times the rod of the Romans. They just kept going until they killed you, grew tired of it, or their commanding officer told them to stop. Besides all the other things that he mentions—frequent hunger, dangers on the sea, dangers from brigands—Paul says he faces the danger of false brothers. He has seen it all.

In other words, he is often hard pressed, perplexed, persecuted, struck down—but not destroyed. He summarizes these experiences in verse 10 of our chapter:

> We always carry around in our body the death of Jesus, so that the life of Jesus may also be revealed in our body.

This is another way of saying that we are supposed to take up our cross and follow Jesus. We are to die to self. Yet, there is a "so that" halfway through verse 10, and another in verse 11:

> For we who are alive are always being given over to death for Jesus' sake, so that his life may also be revealed in our mortal body.

In other words, the appeal is not simply to suffering and sacrifice. There is a recognition that God is no one's debtor. We willingly endure suffering and self-death *so that* the power of the gospel will work through our lives—Christ's resurrection life actually working within us to bring about its own glory and reward.

You recall what Paul says elsewhere in this book (2 Corinthians 12). He has been suffering from what he calls "a thorn in my flesh, a messenger of Satan" (v. 7). He prays earnestly that the Lord will take it away, but the Lord simply says, in effect, "I'm going to add more grace instead." Ultimately, Paul recognizes the superiority of experiencing such divine strength in the context of his own weakness, and he says, "I will boast all the more gladly about my weaknesses, *so that* Christ's power may rest on me" (v. 9).

When I was a boy, there was a lot of emphasis in missionary meetings, missionary calls, and the like on the importance of sacrifice. God knows we need to hear that side of things. We used to sing a song that virtually no one remembers any more:

So send I you to labor unrewarded,
To serve unpaid, unloved, unsought, unknown;
To bear rebuke, to suffer scorn and scoffing.
So send I you to toil for me alone.

So send I you to bind the bruised and broken,
O'er wandering souls to work, to weep, to wake;
To bear the burdens of a world aweary,
So send I you to suffer for my sake.

So send I you to loneliness and longing,
With heart ahung'ring for the loved and known,
Forsaking home and kindred, friend and dear one—
So send I you to know my love alone.

So send I you to leave your life's ambition,
To die to dear desire, self-will resign;
To labor long, and love where men revile you,
So send I you to lose your life in mine.

So send I you to hearts made hard by hatred,
To eyes made blind because they will not see;
To spend, though it be blood, to spend and spare not,
So send I you to taste of Calvary.[2]

Yes, that's right. But it's only half the truth. For although Paul says he is hard pressed, perplexed, persecuted, and struck down, he also says, in 4:10, that it is "*so that* the life of Jesus may also be revealed in our body." And again, verse 11: "*so that* his life may also be revealed in our mortal body." He also says, verse 15: "All this is for your benefit, *so that* the grace that is reaching more and more people may cause thanksgiving to overflow to the glory of God." And again, back in 3:18: "And we all, who with unveiled faces contemplate the Lord's glory, are being transformed into his image with ever-increasing glory, which comes from the Lord, who

---

is the Spirit." Indeed, he insists in 4:17–18: "For our light and momentary troubles are achieving for us an eternal glory that far outweighs them all. So we fix our eyes not on what is seen, but on what is unseen, since what is seen is temporary, but what is unseen is eternal."

These two emphases necessarily hang together. We are crucified with him and we see glory with him. We die to self and we experience more of his life. You cannot have one without the other. They hang together. You do not crave self-sacrifice because you are a masochist. God is no one's debtor. But in following Jesus, who went to the cross, we learn to pick up our crosses and follow him, for that too is part of our gospel mission, knowing full well that as he was vindicated, so we too will reign with him.

So if you want to know what biblical mission looks like, hear this: gospel ministry is characterized by paradoxical death to self and overflowing life in Christ.

What is the biblical basis for missions?

What we find in these verses is not so much an abstract definition of the biblical basis for missions as a mind-expanding depiction of how the mission of gospel ministry works: how it is tied to gospel truth, is discharged with unqualified integrity, reverberates with God's passion to display the glory of his Son Jesus Christ, and is heralded in the context of paradoxical self-death, which, nevertheless, overflows with the transforming life of Christ.

Here is the heart of biblical mission.

WHY THE GREAT COMMISSION IS GREAT

Reaching More and More People

2 CORINTHIANS 4:13–18

David Platt

In a world made up of approximately sixteen thousand people groups, more than six thousand of which are still classified as unreached with the gospel, we read these words in 2 Corinthians 4:13–18:

> Since we have the same spirit of faith according to what has been written, "I believed, and so I spoke," we also believe, and so we also speak, knowing that he who raised the Lord Jesus will raise us also with Jesus and bring us with you into his presence. For it is all for your sake, so that as grace extends to more and more people it may increase thanksgiving, to the glory of God.
>
> So we do not lose heart. Though our outer self is wasting away, our inner self is being renewed day by day. For this light momentary affliction is preparing for us an eternal weight of glory beyond all comparison, as we look not to the things that are seen but to the things that are unseen. For the things that are seen are transient, but the things that are unseen are eternal.

C. T. Studd was a wealthy Englishman, who, upon coming to Christ, sold everything he had so he could take the gospel to the nations. Many sought to dissuade him, but he went anyway, first to China and then to India. At the age of fifty, he decided retirement was not an option for the Christian, so he spent the remaining years of his life proclaiming the gospel in Sudan. He died there, and his grave became a steppingstone for what was known as the Worldwide Evangelization Crusade, which helped spread the gospel across Africa, Asia, and South America. Studd once wrote:

> Believing that further delay would be sinful, some of God's insignificants and nobodies in particular, but trusting in our Omnipotent God, have decided on certain simple lines, according to the Book of God, to make a definite attempt to render the evangelization of the world an accomplished fact. . . . Too long have we been waiting for one another to begin! The time for waiting is past! The hour of God has struck! . . . In God's holy name let us arise and build! . . . We will not build on the sand, but on the bedrock sayings of Christ, and the gates and minions of hell shall not prevail against us. Should such men as we fear? Before the whole world, aye, before the sleepy, lukewarm, faithless, namby-pamby Christian world, we will dare to trust our God, we will venture our all for Him, we will live and we will die for Him, and we will do it with His joy unspeakable singing aloud in our hearts. We will a thousand times sooner die trusting only in our God than live trusting in man. And when we come to this position the battle is already won, and the end of the glorious campaign in sight. We will have the real Holiness of God, not the sickly stuff of talk and dainty words and pretty thoughts; we will have a [real] Holiness, one of daring faith and works for Jesus Christ.[1]

These words summarize my prayer not just for The Gospel Coalition, but for this movement—The Gospel Coalition, Together for

---

[1] Quoted in Norman Grubb, *C. T. Studd: Cricketer & Pioneer* (Fort Washington, PA: CLC Publications, 1933), 119–121.

the Gospel, the Cross student conference—and for the church as a whole in our day. I want to see brothers and sisters coming together from churches in diverse streams and varying denominations with a bedrock focus on the glory of God and the wonder of grace in the gospel, so that gospel celebration, gospel hymns, gospel conferences, gospel books, gospel unity, and gospel centrality would compel a gospel urgency in us. I desire that together we might make a definite attempt, under the sovereign grace of our God, to render the evangelization of the world an accomplished fact.

Now, as I say that, I want to be clear about what I am *not* trying to do. I am not trying to propose a particular utopian vision. I am not trying to posit a particular eschatological position. I am not trying to say that we in this gospel-centered movement, or even we in the Western church alone, can just pull ourselves up by our bootstraps and complete the Great Commission. Nor am I at all trying to say that *we* are ultimately sovereign over when disciples are made in every nation. God is sovereign over all of that. But our sovereign God has given us a specific goal, and it is crystal clear: he has commanded *his people* to make disciples of *all peoples*—all the *ethne* of the world. And he has given us a promise: his very presence and the power of his Spirit to accomplish his purpose. So as we coalesce around this gospel, empowered by his Spirit, I want to urge us not to be content with "the sickly stuff of talk and dainty words and pretty thoughts." Let's "dare to trust our God," let's "venture our all for Him," and let's "live and die for Him." Let's go together with our brothers and sisters around the world after the most difficult- and dangerous-to-reach people groups, and let's "do it with His joy unspeakable singing aloud in our hearts" every step of the way. This, I am convinced, is the heart of the apostle Paul in 2 Corinthians 4 and 5.

Based on 2 Corinthians 4:13–18, I want to exhort those of us who have coalesced around the gospel to live our lives, to lead our families, to preach our sermons, to conduct our conferences, to write our blogs, to publish our books, and to shepherd our churches (Jesus's church) in a definite attempt to render the evangelization of the world (under the sovereign grace of our God) an accomplished fact. That's the *Great* Commission: disciples made and churches multiplied in every nation, among every people group on the planet. *That* is what the gospel compels us to do. Here are three exhortations from this text for a gospel-coalesced people:

1. Believe the Gospel with Deep-Seated Conviction and Proclaim It with Death-Defying Confidence

In 2 Corinthians 4:1–12, Paul explains the power of the gospel message while acknowledging the weakness of the gospel messenger. He describes the affliction and the suffering that accompany gospel ministry. Then, in verse 13, Paul reaches back into the Psalms to describe his motivation for perseverance in gospel mission. Psalm 116, a song of deliverance written by a psalmist who had been saved from what looked like certain death, says, "I believed, even when I spoke: 'I am greatly afflicted'" (v. 10). The psalmist draws a clear correlation between believing and speaking—he believes, and so he speaks. Suffering and affliction cannot stop him from speaking what he believes. According to the psalmist, suffering cannot silence the spirit of faith. And so Paul says that *this* same spirit of faith is in us—even in the midst of affliction and suffering, "we also believe, and so we also speak" (2 Cor. 4:13).

According to Paul, believing automatically leads to speaking. Possession of faith automatically leads to proclamation of faith. You can't disconnect the two, particularly when you consider the content of faith: "knowing that he who raised the Lord Jesus will raise us also with Jesus and bring us with you into his presence" (2 Cor. 4:14). According to Paul, when you believe in the resurrection of Jesus, you proclaim the resurrection of Jesus. There is no such thing as privatized faith in a resurrected Christ. Those who believe the gospel of Jesus proclaim the gospel of Jesus, no matter what it costs.

I believe there is a needed word here for us today. Privatized Christianity is a profound curse across our culture *and* our churches. Multitudes of professing Christians live as if they believe the following:

> Jesus has saved me. Jesus's teachings work for me and my family. But who am I to tell my neighbor or my coworker what he or she should believe? Who am I to go and tell other people in other nations that their beliefs are wrong and my belief is right? And even more, who am I to tell anyone that if they don't believe in what I believe, they'll spend eternity damned in hell?

I tell our church members who struggle with this—from college students to senior adults and everyone in between—that I can identify with this train of thought. I think back to standing one day in a sea of people in the region of North India. If you've never been to India, just think *people*. Lots and lots and lots of people. Approximately 1.2 billion of them, over 600 million of whom live in North India. Crowded streets and urban slums surrounded by seemingly endless villages span the countryside. More people live below the poverty line in India than the entire population of the United States. The church partners with whom my church has worked in India estimate that approximately 0.5 percent of the people in North India are Christians. In other words, 99.5 percent of the people in North India have not believed in Christ for salvation. Now, obviously no one knows that kind of statistic for certain, and I want to be cautious in even suggesting it—but let's assume this statistic for a moment (which, even if it's off, is likely not far off). I looked around one day in that crowded sea of people and thought:

> Who am I to travel all the way over here to tell these people what they need to believe? Who am I to tell them that all of their gods are false, whether they're Hindu, Muslim, Buddhist, Sikh, or any other gods, because Jesus is the only true God? And who am I to tell these 597 million non-Christians (99.5 percent of North India) who surround me at this moment that if they do not turn from their sin and trust in Jesus, then every single one of them will spend eternity in hell?

It felt extremely arrogant, entirely unloving, and uncomfortably brash to claim that 597 million Hindus, Muslims, Buddhists, and Sikhs around me at that moment would go to hell if they didn't confess with their mouths that Jesus is Lord and believe in their hearts that God raised him from the dead (Rom. 10:9–10). And such a claim absolutely would be arrogant, unloving, and brash—unless the claim is true. Isn't this what Paul says? If Jesus didn't rise from the dead, then Christians are to be pitied (1 Cor. 15:19), and the *worst* thing we could do is persuade other people to base their lives on a lie (vv. 14–15). If Jesus didn't rise from the dead, then it's outright foolishness to go around the world telling people that they either need to follow Jesus or face hell.

But if Jesus *did* rise from the dead, if Jesus alone paid the price for man's sin, and if Jesus alone conquered sin, death, and the grave, then going around the world and telling people about Jesus is the *only* thing that makes sense. If Jesus did rise from the dead, then it is the height of arrogance to sit quietly by while 597 million Hindus, Muslims, Buddhists, and Sikhs in North India go to hell. And it's the epitome of hate to not sacrifice our lives to spread this good news among all the people we know and among every people group on the planet. When you believe this gospel, you speak this gospel. When you believe in the resurrection of Christ, you proclaim the resurrection of Christ. Privatized faith in a resurrected King is practically inconceivable.

We believe, and so we speak.

All of us—church members, church leaders, and pastors—need to ask ourselves this question: Do we *really* believe this gospel? Do we really believe this good news, that the sovereign, holy, just, and gracious Creator of the universe has looked upon hopelessly sinful men and women in their rebellion and has sent his Son, God in the flesh, to bear his wrath against sin on the cross and to show his power over sin in the resurrection? He has risen from the dead! We're not talking resuscitation or reincarnation. It wasn't as if Jesus was unconscious before getting a vision of heaven, and then he came back to write a best-selling book about it. We're talking about being killed by crucifixion, wrapped in graveclothes, and put in a tomb, but three days later, the tomb was empty and Jesus was alive. He rose from the dead, and anyone and everyone who repents and believes in him will be reconciled to God forever. Do we believe this?

If we do believe this gospel of the resurrected Christ, then we cannot sit quietly by in our churches while six thousand people groups in the world comprising 2 billion people have never even heard it. We cannot be content to spend our time, our money, and our resources in our lives and in our churches on comfortable plans and temporal possessions when hundreds upon hundreds of millions of people have never even heard the news of the resurrected Christ. We believe, and so we are compelled to proclaim the resurrected Christ to unreached peoples, knowing that as we speak this gospel to them, we will face suffering and affliction.

These six thousand people groups are unreached for a reason—they're hard to reach. All the easy ones have already been evangelized. These people groups are dangerous to reach. These people groups don't want to be reached, and anyone who tries to reach them with the gospel will most certainly be met with suffering and affliction. The more I have studied 2 Corinthians 4:13–18, the more convinced I have become that this text cannot be rightly understood apart from the context of gospel proclamation in difficult, even dangerous places.

Now, I want to be careful here: there's no question that there are truths, principles, and glorious realities in 2 Corinthians 4 that echo throughout Scripture to form a general theology of suffering for the Christian. Without question, there are truths here that bring deep comfort to Christians who are suffering with cancer or other physical maladies, those who are grieving over lost loved ones, and those who are walking through all sorts of suffering in a sinful world. But in this letter, Paul is specifically describing (and, in a sense, defending) the suffering he has experienced as he has proclaimed the gospel in dangerous places among difficult peoples. What Paul is experiencing is not happening to him because he's sitting back on his couch all day or because he's just carrying on business as usual in life and ministry. No, he's going to dangerous places among difficult peoples and speaking the gospel to them, and much (if not most) of his suffering is a direct result of that.

We see the reality of Paul's situation later when he recounts all that he has endured. In 2 Corinthians 11:23–27, he compares himself to those who opposed him:

> Are they servants of Christ? I am a better one—I am talking like a madman—with far greater labors, far more imprisonments, with countless beatings, and often near death. Five times I received at the hands of the Jews the forty lashes less one. Three times I was beaten with rods. Once I was stoned. Three times I was shipwrecked; a night and a day I was adrift at sea; on frequent journeys, in danger from rivers, danger from robbers, danger from my own people, danger from Gentiles, danger in the city, danger in the wilderness, danger at sea, danger from false brothers; in toil and hardship, through many a sleepless night, in hunger and thirst, often without food, in cold and exposure.

All of this is a direct result of proclaiming the gospel throughout Asia. For instance, Paul begins this letter by talking about "the affliction we experienced in Asia," where "we were so utterly burdened beyond our strength that we despaired of life itself" (2 Cor. 1:8). Now, we don't know if this is a reference to the Demetrius riot (Acts 19:21–41), Paul's literal or figurative fighting with "beasts" at Ephesus (1 Cor. 15:32), a severe illness, or some other affliction he faced. Whatever Paul is referring to, it was tied to his proclamation of the gospel in Asia, and it threatened to thwart his proclamation of the gospel to the nations. And it's in *that* context, the context of mission to dangerous places among difficult peoples, that Paul says, "I believed, and so I spoke" (2 Cor. 4:13), knowing that suffering, affliction, and persecution would come, yet "knowing that he who raised the Lord Jesus will raise us also with Jesus" (v. 14).

The principle here, one by no means isolated to this portion of

Scripture, is clear: persecution follows proclamation. Suffering for the gospel accompanies the spreading of the gospel. Think about our brothers and sisters currently in Saudi Arabia, North Korea, and Somalia. If they believe in silence, without saying anything about the gospel, then they can stay below the radar. But if they believe and they speak, the result is drastically different. In the words of one Somali woman I spoke with in the Horn of Africa a few months ago, "If I speak the gospel to the wrong person, they'll slit my throat immediately." As long as Christians stay silent about the gospel, there's no problem. But as soon as Christians start speaking about the gospel, that's a problem. Persecution follows proclamation.

Now, to be clear, I'm not saying that every circumstance in the world is as extreme as Saudi Arabia, North Korea, or Somalia, but I am saying this: if you and I are going to be serious about making disciples among all six thousand unreached people groups, we need to realize it's not going to come without cost—to us, to our families, to our churches, and to the lives and families of the people we lead and love. I think about three couples our church has sent out this year to lead church-planting teams among some of the most dangerous, difficult-to-reach peoples on the planet, and two of these couples had young kids. We gathered around them and prayed for them; it was like the account of Paul and the elders at Ephesus in Acts 20. There was weeping over friends and family members whom we love, for we knew that we were sending them into difficult parts of the Middle East, Central Asia, and North Africa. I told our people that we were not doing this because we had some dark desire to be dangerous. This was simply the reality of engaging unreached peoples. They're not only hard to reach, but many of them are resistant to being reached, and they oppose those who try to reach them.

"Why do we go to them if they're going to resist us?" our people ask. The answer is simple: it's the gospel. We go because God came to us when we were resistant to being reached by him, and he sent his Son to sacrifice his life for our salvation. So it just makes sense for people who possess this gospel to have a death-defying commitment to proclaiming this gospel. As we believe the gospel with deep-seated conviction in our lives, let's proclaim the gospel with death-defying confidence in the world.

The second exhortation flows directly from the first, and it just leaps off the page in 2 Corinthians 4:15.

2. Live to Extend God's Grace among More People and Long to Exalt God's Glory among All Peoples

In 2 Corinthians 4:15, Paul sets forth a twofold goal, a dual aim for ministry. This verse single-handedly sums up the purpose of Christian missions.

For the Sake of People

First, Paul says, "It is all for your sake." All of it—his preaching, suffering, persecution, affliction, and proclamation—is for the Corinthians' sake, so that more and more of them might experience the grace of God. Isn't this what we want our lives to be about? Isn't this what we want our ministries, our churches, and our partnerships among churches to be about—extending the grace of God to more and more people for their sake, so that more and more men and women and boys and girls might know the resurrected Christ? That they might be saved from their sins? That they might be brought from darkness to light? That they might be delivered from everlasting condemnation away from God to experience everlasting communion in the presence of God?

Earlier, I mentioned India, but I don't want to leave a dark picture of India with you. I want to share a story about how the grace of God is extending to more and more people. Travel to Bihar, India, with me. This state in North India is one of the most spiritually and physically impoverished places on the planet. Bihar is about the size of Tennessee; the difference is that Tennessee has six million people, while Bihar has a hundred million! That's a hundred million people spread across forty-five thousand villages. The majority of those people are extremely poor, with millions living in desperate poverty, but not just physically. Bihar is approximately 0.1 percent Christian. Most Indians in Bihar are Hindu. In the particular region we were in, the death rate is about five thousand people per day, which means that every day in this region approximately 4,995 people plunge into an eternal hell, most without ever having heard the gospel. Our church has been working in partnership with brothers and sisters in Bihar, having helped provide training in disciple making and church multiplication to Christians and pastors who live there. A few months ago, I had the privilege of seeing the fruit of that partnership in a humbling, glorious picture of God's grace. My mentor in ministry was with me in Bihar, and his comment at one point on the trip was that this was just about the closest he had ever been to seeing what we see happening in the New Testament two thousand years ago.

We met two brothers named Anil and Hari. Three years ago, living in the middle of spiritual darkness and not seeing any fruit in the gospel, these brothers were at the end of their rope and ready to quit ministry altogether. But at a training session in disciple making, Anil and Hari were encouraged to find a totally unreached village, go into that village, greet people in Jesus's name, and ask if they could pray for the homes there. Truth be told, Anil and Hari didn't think it would do any good, but they thought, "What do we have to lose?" So they went.

In the first village they came to, no one paid them any attention until they had walked through almost the entire village. Then a man came up to them and asked what they were doing. Anil and Hari went through their scripted lines, and as soon as they mentioned the name of Jesus, this man said: "Jesus? I have heard a little about him, and I want to know more. Can you help me?" Anil and Hari looked at each other, looked back at this man, and said, "Yeah, we can help." So the man invited Anil and Hari into his home, and he told them to wait there while he went and brought the rest of his family and some of his friends. When they arrived, they asked Anil and Hari to share with them about Jesus. To make a long story short, within a couple of weeks, about twenty people in that village became followers of Christ, and a church began.

The story gets better. Anil and Hari started mobilizing those new Christians to go and do the same thing in other villages, and they did. Now, three years later, as a result of what happened in that one village, people have come to Christ and churches have begun in 350 villages. We worshiped with these churches.

For a variety of reasons, I get somewhat cynical when I hear numbers like these, particularly from India, but these brothers and the ministry partners we're working with are in touch with these churches and are continually measuring their health. They have a grid that identifies the characteristics of a New Testament church, and they evaluate all these churches through that grid. They visit them and help them to think through how to grow. By God's grace, the churches are multiplying!

God is pouring out his Spirit in Bihar, or at least this region of Bihar. That's not to say it's easy: Anil and Hari have faced all kinds of challenges (from outside the church *and* inside the church) and various afflictions, yet in the middle of it all, the gospel is spreading to more and more people for the sake of more and more villages.

On one occasion in Bihar, as we gathered with one church, the relatively new believers there shared testimonies of how they had come to Christ. One of the men (a new brother in Christ) looked at us and said, "Our village was like hell until we heard the gospel." Paul, as well as Anil and Hari, says, "It is all for your sake—that you might know the grace of God."

For the Sake of God's Glory

But that's not all. Remember, Paul lays out a twofold goal, a dual aim of gospel ministry, and the purpose of Christian missions is far greater than the salvation of souls for eternity (as if that's not enough)!

Notice the last part of 2 Corinthians 4:15: "It is all for your sake, so that as grace extends to more and more people it may increase thanksgiving, *to the glory of God.*" The proper end of missions is not the salvation of souls; the proper end of missions is the glory of God, or, more specifically, thanksgiving to the glory of God. The end of missions is more and more people who are happy in God. Isn't this the cry of the psalmist? "Let the nations be glad and sing for joy. . . . Let the peoples praise you, O God; let all the peoples praise you!" (Ps. 67:4–5). Isn't this the cry of the angel from heaven? "I bring you good news of great joy that will be for all the people" (Luke 2:10). Isn't this the cry of Paul himself, who says that his ambition is to "preach the gospel, not where Christ has already been named," *so that* "Those who have never been told of him will see, and those who have never heard will understand" (Rom. 15:20–21).

Not giving thanks is the problem in the first place. Apart from the gospel, people don't give thanks to God. Romans 1:18 refers to the wrath of God being revealed against sinners for their ungodliness. Paul says in verse 21, "For although they knew God, they did not honor him as God or give thanks to him." Instead of giving thanks to God, sinners follow a different course, as Paul describes in verses 21–25:

> They became futile in their thinking, and their foolish hearts were darkened. Claiming to be wise, they became fools, and exchanged the glory of the immortal God for images resembling mortal man and birds and animals and creeping things.
>
> Therefore God gave them up in the lusts of their hearts to impurity, to the dishonoring of their bodies among themselves, because they exchanged the truth about God for a lie and worshiped and served the creature rather than the Creator, who is blessed forever! Amen.

The problem, Paul says, is that there are scores of people (Gentiles) who aren't giving thanks to God; they're not glorifying God as God. This is why it is Paul's ambition to get the gospel to them. For example, Paul wants to take the gospel to Spain, according to Romans 15:24, and he wants the believers in Rome to help him get there. There are people there who haven't heard the gospel, and they aren't giving thanks to God and thus giving him the glory that he is due.

This desire to see God glorified is what drives us in missions; this is *why* we want to render the evangelization of the world an accomplished fact. It is not because we feel guilty that we have the gospel and they don't. It is not because we feel guilty because we have all these resources and they don't. People ask, "Aren't you just guilting people into going overseas and to unreached peoples?" No. What drives passion for missions among unreached peoples is not guilt, it's glory—glory for our God. Why must we sacrifice our lives and shepherd our churches to penetrate to unreached peoples with the gospel? We do so because we are convinced down to the core of our being that our God deserves the praise not just of a few thousand people groups on the planet; our God deserves the praise of all sixteen thousand people groups on the planet.

In every new member workshop we have in the church I pastor, I start by telling the attendees that Jesus has all authority in heaven and on earth (Matt. 28:18), which means he is worthy of their worship. He is Lord, so we have sacrificed the right to determine the direction of our lives. We give him a blank check. His lordship is why we want members of the church to leave and go all over our city and to cities around North America. Even beyond that:

- This is why we go to Africa: there are more than three thousand animistic tribes in Africa worshiping all kinds of gods and spirits, but Jesus alone is worthy of their worship.
- This is why we go to Japan, Laos, and Vietnam: there are 350 million Buddhists in those countries who are following Buddha's rules and regulations, but Buddha is not worthy of their worship; Jesus alone is worthy of their worship.
- This is why we go to India, Bangladesh, and Nepal: there are 950 million Hindus in those countries who are worshiping more gods than you or I can even fathom, but there is only one who is worthy of their worship, and his name is Jesus.
- This is why we go to China, North Korea, and Cuba: in these communist nations, there are more than a billion people who've

grown up in atheistic philosophies that completely deny the existence of God. We go because there is a God, his name is Jesus, and he is worthy of their worship.

- This is why we go to the Middle East, Central Asia, and North Africa: in these places, there are more than 1.5 billion Muslims who are fasting, giving alms, making holy pilgrimages to Mecca, and praying five times a day to a false god. Yet Jesus died on the cross, rose from the grave, and ascended to heaven as the exalted Lord, and he alone is worthy of all their worship.

A people who believe God is worthy of that kind of glory will give their lives making his glory known.

This is our ultimate aim. This is what we mean by the evangelization of the world. We want to see the fulfillment of the apostle John's vision:

> After this I looked, and behold, a great multitude that no one could number, from every nation, from all tribes and peoples and languages, standing before the throne and before the Lamb, clothed in white robes, with palm branches in their hands, and crying out with a loud voice, "Salvation belongs to our God who sits on the throne, and to the Lamb!" (Rev. 7:9–10)

There it is—the twofold goal, the dual aim, the supreme purpose of missions. This is what makes the Great Commission *great*— salvation for others, which leads to glory for God. As we live to extend God's grace among more people, let's long to exalt God's glory among all peoples.

Everything we've seen so far leads to a third exhortation, which is based on Paul's last three verses in this text:

3. Continually Envision Eternal Glory with God and Joyfully Embrace Earthly Suffering from God

As long as we believe this gospel in our lives, and as long as we proclaim this gospel in this world, our outer self will be "wasting away" (2 Cor. 4:16). We will experience affliction, and we should not be surprised by that. Who really thinks that making disciples of all the nations is an easy task? I think back to 2 Corinthians 4:4–6, where Paul talks about the battle between the god of this world and the God over this world. We're right in the middle, preaching Christ. Do we really think this battle is going to be easy?

I have a dear pastor friend whom I respect deeply, a man who has pastored the same church for about thirty years. He has been passionate about the nations longer than I have been alive. He told me recently that this last year has been his toughest year in ministry, with people in his church resisting the call of God to the nations. When I heard him say that, I was discouraged. I thought: "Really? After thirty years of shepherding the church on mission, things just get harder? Is that really the case?" Then I realized the folly of my thoughts. Do I really think that there will ever be a point in this world when pushing back darkness among the nations will be easy? Ministry will never be easy as long as we are on the front lines.

This should not surprise us, for Jesus promised that it wouldn't be easy. We follow a Savior who sends his disciples out like sheep among wolves (Matt. 10:16). He said: "A disciple is not above his teacher, nor a servant above his master. It is enough for the disciple to be like his teacher, and the servant like his master" (Matt. 10:24–25). And again: "'A servant is not greater than his master.' If they persecuted me, they will also persecute you" (John 15:20). The only possible conclusion we can draw from these words is that our danger in this world increases in proportion to the depth of our relationship with Christ. The only possible exhortation from these words is clear: to all wanting a safe, comfortable, cozy life free from danger in this world, stay away from Jesus.

Paul similarly exhorted the earliest Christians that "through many tribulations we must enter the kingdom of God" (Acts 14:22), for "all who desire to live a godly life in Christ Jesus will be persecuted" (2 Tim. 3:12). This is expected, Peter tells us: "Do not be surprised at the fiery trial when it comes upon you to test you, as though something strange were happening to you" (1 Pet. 4:12). Likewise, Jesus tells his church in Revelation 2:10: "Do not fear what you are about to suffer. Behold, the devil is about to throw some of you into prison, that you may be tested, and for ten days you will have tribulation. Be faithful unto death, and I will give you the crown of life." Revelation 6:10–11 makes clear that there are more martyrs yet to come before the commission of Christ is complete. So this is the unavoidable takeaway from the New Testament: the more passionate we are about spreading the gospel to every people group in the world, the more we will suffer, not because we're *seeking suffering*, but because we're *speaking Christ*, and *suffering for* the gospel accompanies the *spread of* the gospel. And all of this is *from God*. This is not by accident. This is according to his design.

Consider one of the couples we recently sent out from our church. Two of the most poignant moments in my short seven years of pastoring this church both happened with this couple. I remember when they met with our elders about the possibility of becoming a part of our international church-planting internship in order to lead a church-planting team among a particularly dangerous people group. One of our older elders solemnly looked at this young couple, and specifically the young wife, and said, "Do you realize the risk involved in where you want to go, and what that risk means for you and your family?"

I'll never forget how this wife responded. She looked back with humility, compassion, and confidence, and she said in the sweetest, yet most solemn, Southern voice you can imagine: "I believe God's Word is true. And his Word says that his gospel will spread through persecution, hardship, and suffering. And I am good with that." Our room of elders sat silent. No one spoke, and there was not a dry eye in the room. Then, a few weeks later, as her husband was sharing with our church, he said at one point, "I know that some of you think we are being reckless." He was sitting there with his precious wife and two young kids, preparing to go into the heart of an unreached Muslim people group, and he looked at our church and said, "I am convinced that we are in far greater danger from being safe than we are from being reckless in the church today." As I listened to him explain conclusions he had come to based on study in Acts and the epistles of the New Testament, I couldn't help but agree with him. We have made safety a god, not just in our culture, but in the church. We have equated safety with wisdom, and we have sought to ensure safety with our wealth in a way that seems completely foreign to followers of Christ in the New Testament.

I'm not saying that we need to be reckless in going to the nations, but I am saying that there will be great risk in going to the nations, and if we're not willing to take that risk, we will *not* be a part of the accomplishment of the Great Commission. God will pass us by as long as we value safety over obedience. So let us embrace suffering from God, and let us embrace it joyfully.

But how do we do that? The answer is found in the crux of this whole text, the hinge sentence upon which everything in 2 Corinthians 4:13–18 turns. It's at the beginning of verse 16: "So we do not lose heart." It's the same phrase Paul uses in verse 1, and now he sums everything up with it. Though afflicted, perplexed, persecuted, struck down, and always being given over to death, we do not lose heart, the Bible says (2 Cor. 4:8–11). All these sufferings are simply preparing "an eternal weight of glory beyond all comparison" (v. 17). Suffering may be inevitable, but God's purpose is unstoppable.

Consider what the apostle says in other passages:

- "For I consider that the sufferings of this present time are not worth comparing with the glory that is to be revealed to us" (Rom. 8:18).
- "And we know that for those who love God all things work together for good, for those who are called according to his purpose" (Rom. 8:28).
- "We rejoice in our sufferings, knowing that suffering produces endurance, and endurance produces character, and character produces hope, and hope does not put us to shame, because God's love has been poured into our hearts through the Holy Spirit who has been given to us" (Rom. 5:3–5).

- "For it has been granted to you that for the sake of Christ you should not only believe in him but also suffer for his sake" (Phil. 1:29).
- ". . . that I may know him and the power of his resurrection, and may share his sufferings, becoming like him in his death" (Phil. 3:10).

Paul says something similar at the beginning and end of 2 Corinthians:

- "Blessed be the God and Father of our Lord Jesus Christ, the Father of mercies and God of all comfort, who comforts us in all our affliction. . . . For as we share abundantly in Christ's sufferings, so through Christ we share abundantly in comfort too" (2 Cor. 1:3–5).
- "But he [God] said to me, 'My grace is sufficient for you, for my power is made perfect in weakness.' Therefore I will boast all the more gladly of my weaknesses, so that the power of Christ may rest upon me. For the sake of Christ, then, I am content with weaknesses, insults, hardships, persecutions, and calamities. For when I am weak, then I am strong" (2 Cor. 12:9–10).

Suffering may be inevitable, but God's purpose is unstoppable. He's working all of this for our good, for our joy, and ultimately for his glory in the world. Remember, it's not just God's purpose in our lives that's unstoppable; it's God's purpose in the world!

Isn't this the story of the church, starting in Acts 7, as Stephen is stoned and the church first experiences martyrdom? Yet *martyrdom* in chapter 7 fuels *missions* in chapter 8, as the church scatters throughout Judea and Samaria preaching the gospel. Oh, I love how Satan not only acts under divine permission, but actually fulfills divine purposes. Satan strikes down one of God's choicest servants (Acts 7:60), and he thinks he's winning. But in the next verse, everyone is scattered (8:1), and they preach the gospel wherever they go (v. 4). Even better, Luke tells us that Saul was there approving of Stephen's execution (v. 1). So Saul leads in the persecution of

Stephen, which leads to the scattering of believers, which leads to the founding of the church at Antioch (Acts 11:19), which becomes the church that one day sends out Saul (Paul) on global mission (Acts 13:1–3). You can't write a script any better than this. Saul inadvertently starts the church that ultimately sends him out.

Don't lose heart: Satan's strategies to stop the church will ultimately serve to spread the church. And Satan's strategies to inflict earthly pain in your life will ultimately serve to increase eternal glory with your God. This is why Paul, referring to his suffering, can say that "this light momentary affliction is preparing for us an eternal weight of glory beyond all comparison" (2 Cor. 4:17). Paul has told us that suffering is inevitable and that God's purpose is unstoppable, and now he tells us that ultimately our hope is incomparable. Compared to coming glory, present suffering is light and momentary, which doesn't mean easy and painless, particularly not at the time. But in light of all time, our present pain in suffering does not compare with our future weight of glory. The word Paul uses in verse 17 is *hyperbolen* (from which we get *hyperbole*, meaning "exaggeration" in English), which literally means "beyond all measure and proportion."[2] In other words, Paul says to the Corinthian church, and by extension to believers today, "The Great Commission—the gospel going to more and more people to the glory of God—will involve great suffering, but be sure of this: eternity will prove it was worth the price."

So for those who have coalesced around the glory of this gospel, let us coalesce around the accomplishment of this commission. As we believe this gospel with deep-seated conviction in our lives, let's proclaim this gospel with death-defying confidence. As we live to extend God's grace among more and more people, let's long to exalt God's glory among all peoples. And as we continually envision eternal glory with God, let's joyfully embrace earthly suffering from God, knowing that:

---

[2] Walter Bauer, *A Greek-English Lexicon of the New Testament and Other Early Christian Literature*, ed. and trans. William F. Arndt, F. Wilber Gingrich, and Frederick W. Danker [BAGD], 3rd ed. (Chicago: University of Chicago Press, 2000), 1032.

If God is for us, who can be against us? He who did not spare his own Son but gave him up for us all, how will he not also with him graciously give us all things? Who shall bring any charge against God's elect? It is God who justifies. Who is to condemn? Christ Jesus is the one who died—more than that, who was raised—who is at the right hand of God, who indeed is interceding for us. Who shall separate us from the love of Christ? Shall tribulation, or distress, or persecution, or famine, or nakedness, or danger, or sword? As it is written,

> 'For your sake we are being killed all the day long;
> we are regarded as sheep to be slaughtered.'

No, in all these things we are more than conquerors through him who loved us. For I am sure that neither death nor life, nor angels nor rulers, nor things present nor things to come, nor powers, nor height nor depth, nor anything else in all creation, will be able to separate us from the love of God in Christ Jesus our Lord. (Rom. 8:31b–39)

3

THE HEART OF GOD IN THE CALL TO PROCLAIM

*A Joyfully Serious Courage in the
Cause of World Missions*

2 CORINTHIANS 5:1–10

John Piper

Missions is the great and glorious calling of Jesus for the church to make disciples among the remaining unreached peoples of the world. Local evangelism and frontier missions are not the same. Frontier missions is the specialized calling to plant the church in people groups where the church hasn't yet taken root.

The International Mission Board estimates that about 3,100 of these unreached peoples are presently unengaged[1]—that is, no evangelical group yet is pursuing a strategy for planting the church among these peoples.

This is a small number of remaining peoples to reach when compared to the scope of Jesus's church. There are 305 million *evangelicals*[2] in the world. That's 98,000 evangelicals for every

[1] "Unengaged Unreached People Groups," Global Research Department, International Mission Board, http://public.imb.org/globalresearch/Pages/default.aspx, accessed May 6, 2014.
[2] "Status of Global Mission, 2013, in the Context of A.D. 1800–2025," *International Bulletin of Missionary Research*, 37, no. 1 (Jan 2013): 33.

unengaged people group. If 1 percent of those 98,000 were newly called to frontier missions, 980 could be assigned to each of the unengaged peoples. There are 4.6 million Christian *congregations* in the world. That's 1,483 congregations for every unengaged people group. There are 44,000 Christian *denominations* in the world. That's fourteen whole denominations for every unengaged people group. There are 4,900 foreign missions sending *agencies* in the world. That's two whole sending agencies for every unengaged people group. If just 10 percent of the attenders at the Passion, Urbana, and Cru Christmas conferences last year were called to these peoples, we could have three missionaries immediately for every one of these remaining 3,100 peoples. And these gatherings represented an infinitesimal part of the Christian students in the world, especially considering India, China, and South Korea—which, after the United States, are the largest missionary-sending countries in the world.

The remaining task of world missions is not staggering statistically. We can do this if we will. That is a big *if*. The human will is weak when it comes to doing the will of God. The world, the flesh, and the Devil war against the human will to finish the Great Commission. All hell is arrayed against this mission. Therefore, the church can find a thousand good things to do instead of doing this.

So it was no accident that the heart of The Gospel Coalition's missions preconference in 2013 was exposition of Scripture, because faith comes by hearing and hearing by the message of Christ (Rom. 10:17). And the will to reach the unengaged peoples of the world will be carried by faith or not at all.

What I would like to do is stir up your faith in the Lord of the harvest and strengthen your will, that you can actually be a significant part of this and perhaps clarify your own calling. And the way I am going to do that is by focusing your attention on 2 Corinthians 5:1–10. There are some astonishing realities here on which to build your life—and your mission.

Our Text in Context

First, let's see how 2 Corinthians 5:1–10 fits into the larger unit of chapters 4–5. The section begins in 4:1 with Paul saying that he has his ministry of proclamation "by the mercy of God." That text had a huge impact on me when I was twenty-eight years old, without a job, and wondering if God would open something up for me. A great teacher reminded me, "You will have your ministry as much by mercy as you have your salvation by mercy." That was true.

In 2 Corinthians 4:5, Paul says his ministry is to proclaim Jesus Christ as Lord, not himself. In 4:7, he begins to focus on this ministry of proclaiming Jesus as coming from a jar of clay, so that all the glory of its effectiveness will go to God. The rest of chapter 4 describes the weakness of that clay pot. And the chapter comes to an end with Paul exulting that in all this weakness, affliction, and wasting away, he is being renewed and therefore does not grow discouraged. Verse 16: "We do not lose heart."

Awakening Courage

Our text, 2 Corinthians 5:1–10, continues to set forth the ground for that hope-filled attitude in the face of weakness. When the text comes to an end in verse 10, Paul launches his concluding section in verse 11 ("Therefore . . . we persuade others . . ."), which leads to the resounding missionary language of verse 20: "Therefore, we are ambassadors for Christ, God making his appeal through us. We implore you on behalf of Christ, be reconciled to God."

So the function of 2 Corinthians 5:1–10 in the larger unit is to give added reasons for not losing heart in the proclamation of Christ. Or, to put it positively, the aim of this text is to awaken and sustain a joyfully serious courage in the ministry of the Word—or, for our purposes, a joyfully serious courage in the cause of missions.

I will point out four ways that this text accomplishes this aim, and give them four headings: realism, resurrection, reunion, and reward.

Realism

Few things are more disillusioning for Christian life and Christian missions than dashed expectations. One remedy for the disillusionment of shattered expectations is realistic expectations. Missionaries—and all other Christians—need a strong dose of biblical realism, and that is what Paul has been giving since 2 Corinthians 4:7 ("jars of clay" realism). And that is what he gives in 5:1–5:

> For we know that if the tent that is our earthly home is destroyed, we have a building from God, a house not made with hands, eternal in the heavens. For in this tent we groan, longing to put on our heavenly dwelling, if indeed by putting it on we may not be found naked. For while we are still in this tent, we groan, being burdened—not that we would be unclothed, but that we would be further clothed, so that what is mortal may be swallowed up by life. He who has prepared us for this very thing is God, who has given us the Spirit as a guarantee.

Paul pops the bubble of any lingering romanticism or naïveté about this life and ministry in it. First, he says that we live in a tent. He calls the body not a castle, not a fortress, and not even a building, but a tent. Verse 1: "For we know that if the tent that is our earthly home . . ." Again in verse 2: "For in this tent . . ." Again in verse 4: "For while we are still in this tent . . ." The point is that tents are weak against the harsh weather of life. Also, tents are temporary; no one expects a tent to last very long. So we would do well to forget any notion of escaping frailty and transience. That is the point of 4:7 ("jars of clay") and of 4:18 ("the things that are seen are transient"). We do missions in our bodies. And our bodies are as frail and temporary as tents.

Second, he pops the bubble of our unrealistic expectations by saying this tent may be destroyed. Verse 1: "For we know that if the tent that is our earthly home is *destroyed* . . ." It doesn't just become tattered, shabby, and threadbare. It gets destroyed. Adoniram Judson, the first American missionary to leave our shores, buried three wives (Ann, Sarah, and Emily) before he died in his mission to Burma. And all three of his and Ann's children died. The first baby was born dead just as they sailed from India to Burma. The second child, a son, lived seventeen months and died. The third, a girl, lived to be two, outlived her mother by six months, and then died. This is the way it's been since Adam, and this is how the mission will go forward until Jesus comes. Our tents not only become tattered; they can be destroyed.

Third, he pops the bubble of unrealistic expectations by describing not just the objective destruction of the tent but the subjective groaning in the tent. Verse 2: "In this tent we groan . . ." Verse 4: "For while we are still in this tent, we groan, being burdened . . ." We groan not just once in a while, but "while we are in this tent," that is, while we live in these bodies. Being a Christian does not lessen the groaning of being human. And being a missionary does not lessen the groaning of being a Christian. The guilt and hopelessness of the groaning are removed, but the groaning remains. The tent has nerve endings. It has physical and emotional limits. They can break. I know one great veteran missionary whose spouse has valiantly battled seasonally immobilizing depression for decades. In this tent we groan.

Fourth, he pops the bubble of unrealistic expectations by calling the Holy Spirit a down payment. Verse 5: "He . . . has given us the Spirit as a guarantee." "Guarantee" is right, but it misses half the meaning. The Greek word *arrabon* means "payment of part of a purchase price in advance."[3] The point is, it *really* is a down payment, and it is *only* a down payment. Both halves of that meaning are crucial. It *is* a strong word of hope: the full payment of blessing *will* someday be made. But it is also a strong word of realism: *someday*. Not yet. You will bury your babies in Burma.

So the first support Paul gives for a joyfully serious courage in the cause of missions is a strong dose of realism to prevent the disillusionment of false expectations. Tent. Destroyed. Groaning. Down payment.

---

[3] Frederick William Danker, *A Greek-English Lexicon of the New Testament and Other Early Christian Literature*, 3rd ed. (Chicago: University of Chicago Press, 2001).

Resurrection

The second way Paul awakens and sustains a joyfully serious courage in the cause of missions is by proclaiming the resurrection of the body, that is, by promising a beautiful and durable building for those who live in rotting tents. He promises in 2 Corinthians 5 that God will swallow up mortality in life.

Verse 1: "For we know that if the *tent* that is our earthly home is destroyed, we have a *building* . . ." Buildings last; tents don't.

Paul is not talking about a heavenly dwelling between the time we die and when we are raised. He talks about that intermediate state in verses 6–8. But in verses 2–4, he ponders the possibility of being without a body—he calls it being naked or unclothed—and shrinks back from it. A disembodied soul is not the ideal.

He says this twice. Verses 2–3: "In this tent we groan, longing to put on our heavenly dwelling, if indeed by putting it on we may not be found naked." Verse 4: "While we are still in this tent, we groan, being burdened—not that we would be unclothed, but that we would be further clothed, so that what is mortal may be swallowed up by life."

"Not be found naked" in verse 3 corresponds to "not that we would be unclothed" in verse 4. Both verses refer to what it would be like to die before resurrection day. Paul is declaring loud and clear: *the ultimate Christian hope is not release from the tent.* Mere release is nakedness. We were not made for bodiless existence. That is not our final destiny.

Rather, we are destined to be swallowed up by life (v. 4b), and Paul lays it down as a rock-solid certainty that this will happen because "He who has prepared us for this very thing is God, who has given us the Spirit as a guarantee" (v. 5). He uses the same logic in Romans 8:11: "If the Spirit of him who raised Jesus from the dead dwells in you, he who raised Christ Jesus from the dead will also give life to your mortal bodies through his Spirit who dwells in you." God made us for this—not bodiless existence, but life in a glorious resurrection body. He is preparing us for this in all our trials. And he has given us a down payment of resurrection life in the Holy Spirit.

And if we wonder what the new body will be like, he tells us three things. First, it will be like a building, not a tent, and God is the builder. Verse 1: "We have a building from God."

Second, it will be like a house not made with hands. Verse 1: "a building from God, a house not made with hands." I cannot help thinking that Paul is alluding here to Jesus's resurrection body, because both the word *destroy* and the phrase "not made with hands" in 2 Corinthians 5:1 are in Mark 14:58, where Jesus is quoted as saying, "I will *destroy* this temple that is made with hands, and in three days I will build another, *not made with hands*." We know Paul thought of our new bodies as like Jesus's body because of Philippians 3:21: Jesus "will transform our lowly body to be like his glorious body." So Paul promises that all the groaning tent dwellers will get new bodies like Jesus's glorious body.

Then, third, he calls it eternal, and he says it is in the heavens— which I take to mean that it is kept safely in the mind and hand of God in the heavens. Second Corinthians 5:1b: "We have a building from God, a house not made with hands, *eternal in the heavens.*"

Being a missionary has always been very risky for this tent we live in. Weariness, disease, torture, and death have been very present realities. And more often than we know, the profound confidence of the resurrection of this familiar old tent overclothed with life, glory, and eternal, building-like stability has sustained the missionary cause in the terrible prospects of the Colosseum, the jungle, and the hostile city.

An old Scottish Christian objected to young John Paton's plan to go as a missionary to the South Sea Islands. "You'll be eaten by Cannibals," he said. Paton responded:

> Mr. Dickson, you are advanced in years now, and your own prospect is soon to be laid in the grave, there to be eaten by worms; I confess to you, that if I can but live and die serving and honoring the Lord Jesus, it will make no difference to me

whether I am eaten by Cannibals or worms; and in the Great Day my resurrection body will arise as fair as yours in the likeness of our risen Redeemer.[4]

Reunion

The third way Paul awakens and sustains a joyfully serious courage in the cause of missions is by assuring the tent dwellers that there will be a reunion with Christ between death and the resurrection, and that this "naked" state with Jesus (though it is not our final destiny) is better than groaning in these tents—better than life here and now in our bodies:

> So we are always of good courage. We know that while we are at home in the body we are away from the Lord, for we walk by faith, not by sight. Yes, we are of good courage, and we *would rather be away from the body and at home with the Lord.* (2 Cor. 5:6–8)

Verse 8 is extremely important: "We would rather be away from the body and at home with the Lord." It protects against a very discouraging misunderstanding of verse 4. There Paul says that we do not want to be unclothed but further clothed. If you had only that verse, you might infer that Paul considers only two good options: life here in the tent or life in the resurrection body. You might think that the prospect of being unclothed—bodilessness between death and resurrection—is totally undesirable. But he does not say that. And in verse 8, he explicitly denies it.

He *does* want to be bodiless—*if* he can be with Jesus: "We *would rather* be away from the body and at home with the Lord." He says the same thing in Philippians 1:23: "My desire is to depart and be with Christ, for that is far better."

So to any missionary who has lost a believing loved one—a funeral just before he or she left the country or the burial of three

---

[4] James Paton, *John G. Paton, Missionary to the New Hebrides* (Fearn, Ross-shire, Scotland: Christian Focus, 2009), 56.

wives overseas—there is this wonderful confidence: the loved ones are not waiting for the resurrection in a worse situation than if they had stayed. No. It is far better. Where are they? They are at home with the Lord.

Twice in 2 Corinthians 5:6–8, Paul sounds the note of courage. Verse 6: "So we are always of good courage." And verse 8: "Yes, we are of good courage." That is why I said his aim is to awaken and sustain joyfully serious courage in the cause of missions.

Realism now. *Resurrection* as a glorious outcome. And *reunion* if we die before Christ comes. This is the ground of joyful courage in the cause of missions.

Reward

The reason I chose to say that Paul is awakening and sustaining joyfully *serious* courage in the cause of missions is because of verses 9 and 10. So we turn finally to these verses under this fourth and final heading:

> So whether we are at home or away, we make it our aim to please him. For we must all appear before the judgment seat of Christ, so that each one may receive what is due for what he has done in the body, whether good or evil. (2 Cor. 5:9–10)

I draw out the word *serious* from these verses because, in the next verse, Paul draws out the word *fear*. Verse 11: "Therefore, knowing the fear of the Lord [that is, in view of the judgment seat of Christ, there is in us a very serious awe, reverence, and trembling, and so], we persuade men."

Fear Compatible with Good Courage

The "fear" that Paul refers to in verse 11, because of the judgment in verse 10, is perfectly compatible with the "good courage" in verses 6 and 8; the down payment of the Spirit in verse 5; the assurance that we have an eternal house in verse 1; and the "we do not lose heart" in 4:16. It's a fear of the Lord that in no way keeps

Paul from saying in 5:8, "We would rather be away from the body and at home with the Lord."

The judgment of believers by the Lord Jesus (and it is believers who are in view in the "we must all appear" of verse 10, because of the link with verse 9) awakens in Paul a kind of fear that does not push him away from Jesus but draws him in. He embraces it. He wants it, because this is the path to Christ.

Peter described this fear in the same kind of connection, perfectly compatible with trust in a loving Father. First Peter 1:17: "If you call on him as Father who judges impartially according to each one's deeds, conduct yourselves with fear throughout the time of your exile." Your judge is your Father, so have a joyful fear. Luke describes the early church experiencing this kind of happy fear: "And walking in the fear of the Lord and in the comfort of the Holy Spirit, [the church] multiplied" (Acts 9:31). For Paul, Peter, and the early church, "the fear of Christ" (as Paul calls it in Ephesians 5:21 NASB) was a serious, sobering expectation of judgment that they embraced as good, healthy, strengthening, and motivating.

Fear Motivating Holiness

Two chapters later, Paul makes the fear of God the motive of Christian holiness: since God promises (2 Cor. 6:18) to be your Father, he says, "[bring] holiness to completion in the fear of God" (7:1).

What is it about the judgment seat of Christ that awakens this holy, motivating fear? We will appear before the judgment seat of Christ "so that each one may receive what is due for what he has done in the body, whether good or evil" (5:10).

I think the best commentary on this judgment from Jesus on our good and evil is 1 Corinthians 3. Paul refers to himself and Apollos: "He who plants and he who waters are one, and each will receive his wages according to his labor" (v. 8). Then Paul illustrates how that labor of building on the foundation of Christ can be rewarded or not:

If anyone builds on the foundation with gold, silver, precious stones, wood, hay, straw—each one's work will become manifest, for the Day will disclose it, because it will be revealed by fire, and the fire will test what sort of work each one has done. If the work that anyone has built on the foundation survives, he will receive a reward. If anyone's work is burned up, he will experience loss, though he himself will be saved, but only as through fire. (vv. 12–15)

There is reward for good building on the foundation. The experience of loss follows bad building on the foundation. This corresponds to 2 Corinthians 5:10: "That each one may receive what is due for what he has done in the body, whether good or evil."

From this awesome scene of rewards and losses, Paul draws this conclusion: "So whether we are at home or away, we make it our aim to please him" (2 Cor. 5:9). He says this "because" we must all appear before the Judge. Two of the great motives of the happy, sober, serious Christian soul are the fear of experiencing loss at the judgment seat of Christ and the joy of receiving our reward for pleasing the Lord. Without faith, it is impossible to please the Lord (Heb. 11:6)—and so the works that are rewarded are the works that come from faith (Rom. 1:5; 16:26; 2 Thess. 1:11; Heb. 11:8), and the works that endure loss are out of step with faith and the gospel (Gal. 2:14).

These Are the Goers and Senders

In summary, then, Paul is modeling, awakening, and sustaining a joyfully serious courage in the ministry of the Word—in the cause of world missions. Joyfully serious and courageous missionaries are protected from disillusionment by the realism of our groaning in this tent. They are filled with joyful and confident hope by the promise of someday being overclothed with eternal and glorious resurrection bodies. They have unshakeable good courage because if they die before the resurrection, there will be a reunion at home with the Lord, which is far better than life in this tent. And they are a cheerfully serious band, knowing the fear of Christ because they will face him to receive rewards or losses for what they have done.

This is the kind of people—radical goers and senders—God is building and calling for the finishing of the task of world evangelization among the unreached peoples of the earth for the glory of Christ. I pray you will be one of them.

4

BEING AMBASSADORS FOR CHRIST

The Ministry of Reconciliation

2 CORINTHIANS 5:11–21

J. Mack Stiles

My life is filled with cross-cultural relationships. The place where I live, Dubai, may be the only city in the world where only ten percent of the residents are citizens, while the rest are from elsewhere: Africa, Asia, Europe, North and South America, and, of course, other parts of the Middle East.

If you had told me when I was growing up that my life would be filled with people from around the world or that I would live in the heart of the Middle East, I probably would have laughed. I grew up in a small town in western Kentucky called Owensboro: a friendly, rural, sleepy place nestled in a broad crook of the massive Ohio River. Growing up in Owensboro was a bit like growing up in the Shire—filled with wonderful people, but a bit isolated from the rest of the world.

Back in Owensboro, if you had asked me my view of Arab people (not that anyone ever did), I would have said, from what I had seen on TV, that all Arabs were Muslims, all Arabs owned guns, and all Arabs would happily shoot Americans.

I left Owensboro many years ago, never to return. As I joyfully followed God into cross-cultural ministry, doors opened to places such as Kenya, Guatemala, and Tunisia. In Tunisia, we partnered with the University of Tunis to place American students in the homes of Arab students who were English majors. It was a summer program of friendship, cultural awareness, and times of sharing faith.

There in Tunisia, I discovered the Arab view of Americans: all Americans were Christians, all Americans owned guns, and all Americans would happily shoot Arabs. Apparently we had been looking at each other through similar TV lenses.

It was also in this program that I met Hatem, an English major from the University of Tunis. Hatem was a man full of fun and competition, and we developed a friendly rivalry.

One bright, sunny day in Tunisia—it was always a bright, sunny day in Tunisia—Hatem took us to the beach. Not just any beach—this was a proper Muslim beach, far from the cavorting, decadent Europeans and Americans. Here Arab families set up large tents with tables full of food. Rotund grandmothers sat fully covered in the sand, overseeing the children as they splashed around in the crystal-clear Mediterranean water.

Hatem and I splashed around, too, until I spied a sandbar out a ways from shore. "Come on Hatem, I'll race you to the sandbar," I said.

"No," replied Hatem, "I need to go take a cigarette."

"Well, okay, you take care of your nicotine fit," I chided. "I'll meet you out there later."

I began to swim at a leisurely pace to the sandbar, while Hatem swam back to shore, or so I thought.

Moments later, I saw a figure underneath me. It was Hatem trying to beat me out to the sandbar! He was taking strong underwater strokes, but I quickened my pace and shadowed him on the surface. He broke the surface with his back to me. What an opportunity!

I grabbed him in a perfect headlock, took him under, and brought him back up, coughing and splashing. For good measure, I dunked him again. I was laughing; he was sputtering. I spun him around, grinning and . . . it wasn't Hatem! It was a very frightened Tunisian who knew that an American had come to kill him personally.

"I'm so sorry," I stammered. He didn't speak English. As I yammered, his fear increased. He began backing up to the shore, arms spinning and legs pumping, all the while keeping his saucerlike eyes on me.

As I followed him to shore, I had an out-of-body experience: I spied his entire extended family pouring from one of the tents. I imagined the headlines in the newspaper the next day: "American Infidel Terrorist Dispatched by Godly Muslim Family on Bizerte Beach."

I needed help—someone to speak the language, someone willing to stand between two warring factions in an attempt to explain a situation, someone to deliver my message. I needed an ambassador.

Guess who showed up? Hatem, smoking his cigarette. He wandered up to see what all the commotion was about. "Hey, what is going on?" he asked as he blew out a puff of smoke.

"Hatem!" I said as I grabbed his arm. "Here, tell these people what happened."

Fortunately for me, and fortunately for my wife and children, Hatem thought this case of mistaken identity was hilarious. As he explained what had just happened, tears streamed down his face. Fortunately, the family found this story hilarious, too. I was never sure if it was because of the way Hatem embellished the story or simply because of the absurdities of it all, but regardless, I was invited in for lunch. As I loaded my plate with briks and couscous garnished with harissa, the men of the family slapped me on the back and told me in broken English that it was a good thing that Hatem had showed up when he did.

Ambassador Hatem! He may have saved my life (though it's more likely he saved me a dental bill) by simply explaining the truth in a way that was understood. There was reconciliation and friendship—and we even got a free lunch.

Second Corinthians 5:11–21 contains some themes similar to those in my beach encounter. It is best known for the image of an ambassador, the person who stands between two warring factions with a message that could avert death. It is a passage saturated with the gospel:

> Therefore, knowing the fear of the Lord, we persuade others. But what we are is known to God, and I hope it is known also to your conscience. We are not commending ourselves to you again but giving you cause to boast about us, so that you may be able to answer those who boast about outward appearance and not about what is in the heart. For if we are beside ourselves, it is for God; if we are in our right mind, it is for you. For the love of Christ controls us, because we have concluded this: that one has died for all, therefore all have died; and he died for all, that those who live might no longer live for themselves but for him who for their sake died and was raised.
>
> From now on, therefore, we regard no one according to the flesh. Even though we once regarded Christ according to the flesh, we regard him thus no longer. Therefore, if anyone is in Christ, he is a new creation. The old has passed away; behold, the new has come. All this is from God, who through Christ reconciled us to himself and gave us the ministry of reconciliation; that is, in Christ God was reconciling the world to himself, not counting their trespasses against them, and entrusting to us the message of reconciliation. Therefore, we are ambassadors for Christ, God making his appeal through us. We implore you on behalf of Christ, be reconciled to God. For our sake he made him to be sin who knew no sin, so that in him we might become the righteousness of God.

Though many things could be said about this passage, I want to highlight five marks of an ambassador for Christ: his motivation (vv. 11–15); his view of people (vv. 16–17); his view of the world

(vv. 18–19); his view of his role (v. 20); and his focus on God's gospel work (v. 21).

An Ambassador's Motivation (vv. 11–15)

Fear, love, and conviction should mark our motivation for sharing our faith.

Paul says our first motivation for persuading people is the fear of God. Verse 11 ("Therefore, knowing the fear of the Lord . . .") flows logically from the statement in verse 10 that judgment is coming for all people. Put another way, the Christian ambassador understands what is at stake. Not only do we know judgment is coming, we are also aware that much of the world does not usually think about the final judgment or even believe it—as if not believing something could make it go away.

So we want to persuade people, not bludgeon them, manipulate them, talk louder than them, or outargue them. We speak the truth plainly to persuade them.

Paul knows that many in his day see a statement of truth about something invisible as arrogance. Similarly, people in our relativistic world see any pronouncement of truth as arrogant and proud; some things have not changed much since Paul's day. But Paul turns the argument on its head by saying that, though the world may interpret his conviction as pride, the Corinthians can actually take pride in his evangelism because they know his heart is right (v. 12).

Paul anticipates another negative interpretation of evangelism: people will think him crazy (v. 13). People acting on their convictions are often written off as crazy. But Paul says he is not controlled by mental illness; rather, he is controlled by the love of Christ (v. 14). Christ's love compels Paul, and us.

What a beautiful thought. We are controlled by the love of God. We are like star-struck lovers, people who are often construed as crazy, too. Have you talked to a person about to be married concerning the person he or she loves? If I've never met the fiancé or fiancée, I fully expect him or her to levitate upon entering the room. That's what love does to us. Even more, for those who love Jesus, his love compels us.

I hope you were able to read the earlier chapter by David Platt. When you see his passion for the lost world, do you get the idea he's a little crazy, a bit on the edge? You know why? Because it's true. His passion has a crazy love to it that the world simply can't understand. David is a tenderhearted brother filled with crazy love that comes from a deep understanding of the coming judgment. I know how he feels. I've stood in the main square in the city of Lucknow, India, looked out over masses of people, contemplated their eternal suffering, and felt a bit crazy about the need to tell them, all of them, about the salvation of God.

But we don't just *feel* crazy at times. There are times, when we tell and live the truth, that we *look* crazy as well. People thought that about Paul, and they will think it about us. But remember, those people don't know what we know about Jesus—especially about his love.

I banged my "For Sale" sign in the front yard of my house the day after 9/11 to head for the Middle East. Our plans had been set for months before the move, but no one would have said a word if we had changed our minds. However, we were convinced that the response of the church to the events of 9/11 must be not military, but missionary. So we moved when the home sold (the next day). My neighbors thought I was out of my mind. I see why they thought that, but it's been the greatest privilege of my life.

There is one more motivation: conviction of truth. As Paul says in verse 14, we have concluded something: Jesus died for all who repent and come to him. We have concluded that sins can be forgiven and that reconciliation with God is possible through the death of Jesus!

I was on a panel at a student conference in Australia, in front of a couple of thousand students, and the question came to me: "Why would you do ministry in the Middle East?"

There are a number of ways I could have answered, but I said:

"Because I really believe this guy rose again from the dead. I'm convinced by the life, death, and resurrection of Jesus."

This conclusion, this conviction of truth, leads us to the understanding in verse 15 that Christ's death was for the sake of the lost. Therefore, those of us who are alive to God don't live for ourselves. We step out of our safe worlds to persuade others. We don't hide from evangelism; we are committed, motivated, and driven to boldness, and even seeming craziness, for those who are lost and without hope in the world.

So in verses 11–15, Paul lists three motivations of an ambassador: the fear of God, the love of Christ, and the conviction of the truth. This potent combination propels us out in ministry to serve others by sharing our faith with a crazy-bold love.

An Ambassador's View of People (vv. 16–17)

Paul says an ambassador who is motivated correctly sees people correctly (v. 16). We give up our TV views. We reject sinful views, fleshly views, and worldly and racist understandings of people. Paul is confronting our natural human tendency to see with worldly eyes.

Paul warns those to whom he is writing even about viewing Jesus with worldly eyes. The same warning applies today. We hear wrong and worldly things every time someone says Jesus was a great moral teacher, that he was just a man, or even that he was a great prophet. No, Jesus is divine, he is God incarnate, and anything less damns him with faint praise. Paul's point is that if we see Jesus that way, how much more likely are we to see others through "TV lenses" and not the eyes of God.

To view people correctly is a situational challenge; it depends on whether they are people we like or don't like. On the one hand, there's no such thing as a "mere mortal," as C. S. Lewis reminded us.[1] All people have the mark of the divine, being created in the image of God. That's why all people have value and worth. So ambassadors check their tendency to hate those they don't like.

---

[1] C. S. Lewis, *The Weight of Glory* (New York: Macmillan, 1949), 19.

At the same time, Christians understand all unsaved people to be sinners and without Christ, enemies of God. We've all been marked by original sin. As G. K. Chesterton says, "Certain new theologians dispute original sin, which is the only part of Christian theology which can really be proved."[2] Chesterton believed that all we need to do to find that proof is look at the last three thousand years of human history. Ambassadors check their tendency to glorify people whom they admire, knowing that every human is fallen and sinful.

But even more than just putting to death human understandings in our hearts, we must put on the most important corrective lenses we can. In verse 17, Paul says we understand the potential of what divinely created but fallen enemies of God can become: new creations, that is, forgiven, restored, and redeemed creations in Christ.

One of the greatest joys in life is to see new creation happen to those we know and love, those who have come to faith and are growing in Christ. I had been praying for my sister for twenty years, and I was tempted to despair that she would ever know God. But one night, after some trying times in her life, I walked her through the gospel message, and to my great amazement, she responded. She had been so hard and distant from God. But when she came to Jesus, her life was radically transformed. She was filled with the love of Jesus. I have watched her become a tenderhearted new creation in Christ. It's a miracle.

It was easy to think that Linda would never come to faith. That can be true of many friends or family members who seem difficult to reach with the gospel. How easy it can be to write them off, saying there are just too many obstacles to reaching them with the gospel. Is that you? Are there people in your life whom you think will never come to Christ? Do you think they are too sinful? Too hard-hearted? Too isolated? Too distant?

Perhaps they look like they have everything they need. Maybe

---

[2] G. K. Chesterton, *Orthodoxy*, Moody Classics (Chicago: Moody, 2013), 11.

you know non-Christians who live lives that seem better than yours as a believer, and you're tempted to think they don't need God. Don't believe it for a minute. Remember the joy of seeing people redeemed as new creations in Christ. You cannot make the decision that someone is too far from God. To see people correctly is to see that the hardest person can become a new creation in the power of God. That's what it means to view people correctly. And it's not just friends and family members. It's happening all over the world.

An Ambassador's View of the World (vv. 18–19)

We have said that an ambassador is rightly motivated to reach out and that an ambassador has his vision of people aligned with God's view of people. An ambassador also has a right view of the gospel message for the world: it's a universal message.

Paul says in verse 19 that God is reconciling the world. That's because, in the gospel, we have a global message. Paul is saying that any person has the ability to come to Jesus, regardless of background. He is confronting the idea that our message is only for certain types of people in the world.

I live in a land that claims Jesus is not the Son of God and that God has no partners. It's trumpeted five times a day from every mosque in the land. Though Muslims certainly honor Jesus more than much of the Western world, to deny that Jesus is the Son of God is to cut the heart out of Christianity. With such a constant avalanche of misinformation, I'm tempted to despair.

But there are no barriers to God or his message. God is the one doing this, not any of us. And reconciliation is happening now around the world because the gospel is a universal message. Our sovereign Lord is at work.

Nastaran is a good friend and colleague in ministry. She's an Iranian who grew up in Tehran. At seventeen, she was a good Muslim girl: she had never seen a Bible, never sung a hymn, and never been inside a church. But one day, as she was taking a shower, she heard a voice say, "I'm going to wash you of your sin."

She didn't know who that was, so she went to the mosque and asked her iman about the voice. Her iman said, "That was Jesus, he is the only prophet who talks that way." Nastaran said, "Thank you," and went home. Not long after this, a woman came to Nastaran with the message of the gospel. Nastaran was ready to hear, and received it with joy. So started an amazing journey of faith and ministry, along with her husband, Yuna.

Now, this is not a story that got many pats on the back in Iran. God's voice in Nastaran's life was the start of a life of humiliation, jail, deportation, and exile. Both Yuna and Nastaran grieved deeply when their pastor, Pastor Hike—the one who had baptized them— was murdered for his faith. Eventually, they, too, were arrested for their faith, and they expected to die, just as Hike had. Yuna says the hardest thing he's ever had to do was watch his wife under interrogation, yet, he says, "She was so brave for the gospel."

Nastaran's testimony was so powerful to the interrogator that when Yuna said to him, "You know all you need to know about the gospel, and you just might become a Christian," the interrogator replied, "I just might do that."

You might be tempted to think that the message of the gospel is somehow for only a small corner of the world, or perhaps for a certain kind of person. But remember, there are no such barriers to God and his message.

I had an interesting conversation with Nastaran. We were talking about the call of Jesus to go to the ends of the earth, and she told me that when she thought about the ends of the earth, especially about the hardest and most difficult corners of the world, the place she had the hardest time believing God could break open was the world of American suburban housewives. One person's "end of the earth" is another person's home, I guess.

What about you? Do you see people from other faith backgrounds and think that no one can get to them? Do you see people of other faith backgrounds and set aside any hope that they could hear the message of faith? It's not true. Don't lose heart. The message of the gospel, this universal message, is moving around the world across all barriers; this message can rescue anyone from eternal judgment, as God calls his people from all the nations of the world.

An Ambassador's View of His Role (v. 20)

Paul is making a case not just for an ambassador's motivation, how an ambassador views people, or how an ambassador views the world. He wants to make a case for how we as Christians see our role in the world. That's what the image of ambassadorship is about.

Paul says in verse 20, "We are ambassadors for Christ, God making his appeal through us." He carefully chooses the image of ambassadorship to make sure we understand our role. Think about it: ambassadors exist to deliver a message. According to Paul, when you sit down for coffee, if a spiritual topic comes up and you begin to share with a friend about Jesus, you represent the foreign power of the kingdom of God. I think this is so mind-blowing that we often don't believe it to be true.

But there are certain responsibilities that come with ambassadorship. First, ambassadors must get the message right. History is filled with horrible outcomes when ambassadors muffed their messages. Christians need to have the message of the gospel firmly fixed in their minds. When I ask the average churchgoing person what the message of the gospel is, I'm amazed at how inarticulate some people can be. Do you have in your head the basic message of the gospel?

Second, ambassadors are not at liberty to change the message. Don't "nice up" the message; deliver it as given. Some want to air-condition hell or ignore God's judgment altogether. Others deliver a message that is more therapy than gospel. Often people forgo discussion about sin or repentance.

Finally, ambassadors cannot leave the message undelivered. Perhaps this is our greatest problem. We have become so fearful about offending, so worried about being rejected, that we don't say anything at all. We need to slay our fears of evangelism and remember the fear of God. We play for him, not the crowd.

By the way, ambassadors, by definition, don't live at home. They are wanderers in the world. That doesn't mean that all Christians need to move to different lands; rather, we shouldn't make this world our home. The Christian should always be a bit uneasy with the world.

At this point in the text, Paul calls out the message. He says, "We implore you on behalf of Christ, be reconciled to God" (v. 20b). To some, this might sound as if Paul is calling to the Corinthians to be reconciled to God. But for all the problems in the church at Corinth, they were Christians. Actually, Paul is shouting out the message we announce as ambassadors to the world: "We implore you, we beg you, be reconciled to God." This is Paul's life message.

One of the most important things I've learned about evangelism in my life is that our pronouncement of the gospel message should be in everything we are and do.

In the book of Galatians, Paul recounts how he rebuked Peter. It must have taken some clear thinking and a strong heart: small Paul rebuked the rock of the church, Peter. On the surface, the reason was an issue about food and fellowship. But the principle Paul understood to be at stake was the proper relationship of the gospel and the law: he says that Peter was not living in *line with the gospel* (Gal. 2:14). Most people think of the gospel message as the message that gets us saved. Paul understood that the gospel is the measure of all of life. Therefore, don't segregate the gospel. It's the A–Z of the Christian life, not just the ABC's. We shouldn't think of the gospel only in the category of evangelism, leaving it out of other segmented areas of the Christian life. This is unfortunately common. Don't untether the gospel from marriage, child rearing, leadership, or anything you do as a believer.

Here's an example of an occasion when all this came together in my mind. To our great surprise, student ministry on the Dubai campuses began to flourish. Bible studies were filling up, and student contacts on various campuses asked if we could help them. I decided it was time for student leadership training. So I worked up a curriculum and invited our best student leaders for a weekly meeting of about twenty in the living room of my house. Most of these students were young believers and few of them had any grounding in the Bible, but all were eager. At our first meeting, the living room hummed with excitement.

But there was one problem. There on my couch sat Akil, a Hindu. So I went to his friend, Nisin, another student leader, and asked him what Akil was doing at a Christian leadership gathering. Nisin reported that Akil just wanted to learn more about leadership. Maybe he wanted to put it on his resume or something.

"Listen, Nisin," I said, "Akil is a nice guy, I like him, but this is our *Christian* leadership meeting, and it's not going to make sense to him."

Nisin said, "Well, maybe I'll talk to him if I get a chance," which meant he wasn't going to talk to him, and sure enough, week by week, Akil was there on the front row of the group, quiet but attentive. Finally, I was so bothered by this, I approached Akil myself. "Hey, Akil," I said, "I need to talk to you about something."

He said, "Oh, I need to talk with you about something, too."

I said, "Okay, you go first."

"Well," he said, "I've become a Christian!" His eyes were shining.

"You did?" I said, rather ungraciously. "How did that happen?"

"It's funny," said Akil, "I was coming because I thought that maybe I could learn something about leadership for business or something." (Later, I found out he also had his eye on an attractive young student named Shebnita.) "But as I listened, I realized that you weren't talking about business leadership principles, but about the gospel and how leadership flows out of the gospel. So last week, I repented of my unbelief and put my trust and faith in Christ alone to save me."

There was an awkward pause as I stared blankly at Akil. Then he asked, "What did you want to talk with me about?" I pointed my finger in the air and then said, "Nothing; never mind."

I went back to Nisin and said, "I'm sorry, brother, forgive me, please keep asking the Hindus to come to our Christian leadership gatherings."

Somehow I had concluded that there is a point at which we move on from the gospel. But because the students were so young and so new to the faith, I was working hard to show the leaders how their leadership sprang from the gospel. So the gospel was carefully integrated into every section of teaching. Hearing the gospel in the leadership lessons was how Akil came to Jesus, and that is how I saw the need for understanding the way the gospel informs all of life.

It would have been easy to leave out the gospel if the leaders had been older and more mature in the faith, but in one sense, it is almost more important for older Christians to make sure all they do is tied into gospel thinking. We need to make sure the gospel is in all we do, as some who are listening can be saved.

Perhaps you're like Akil and are "listening in" as you read. Maybe as you read, it is dawning on you that you are alienated from Christ. You should know that this message is for you, too. See yourself through God's eyes: you are divinely created and yet cut off from God because of your sin and rebellion. But understand your potential, too: you can be reconciled to a loving God, our Father, who sent his Son to pay the penalty for your sins on the cross so that you might be forgiven of sin and have peace with God. What's required of you is not to earn his favor, but to repent of sin, especially the sin of unbelief, and turn to the resurrected Jesus in complete trust and faith, just like Akil.

I want to be like Paul—to be an ambassador with a message to shout out: "Be reconciled to God!"

An Ambassador's Focus on God's Gospel Work (v. 21)

We've seen that an ambassador is motivated in love, sees people as God sees them, and desires to reach all people around the world, clearly understanding the role of an ambassador of the gospel. Finally, an ambassador does these things with a focused understanding of what Jesus has done in the gospel.

Paul says in 2 Corinthians 5:21, "For our sake he made him to be sin who knew no sin, so that in him we might become the righteousness of God." Much ink has been spilt on verse 21. That's because, in just a few brief words, this verse touches on two major theological ideas—substitutionary atonement and imputed righteousness—that are at the heart of the gospel. Paul here gives a behind-the-scenes look at what God did on the cross, helping us see how God purchased for us forgiveness and righteousness.

The words *substitutionary* and *imputed* both point to a righteousness that comes from outside ourselves. It's given, not earned. In other words, the righteousness of a Christian, contrary to the understanding of other religions in the world, comes to us from God. To try to earn our own righteousness is self-righteousness. And besides being impossible, that effort is odious to God. Most of us don't like self-righteous people all that much ourselves. We need a God-given righteousness—a pleasing, sweet-smelling, and pure righteousness.

But substitutionary atonement and imputed righteousness are distinct ideas, too. So let's take them one at a time.

To atone for sin means to pay for it. Much of the world thinks you pay for your sin on your own. It might be done by harsh treatment of the body or by a point system in which good deeds outweigh the bad, but it's always something we do. Substitutionary atonement, on the other hand, is God atoning for you. The Christian understanding is that our sin is too heinous, our ability too weak, and God's holiness too pure for us to be able to atone for ourselves. We need the provision of God, the substitute he provided—his own Son.

This is a consistent theme throughout the Bible. Sacrifices in the Old Testament were to atone for sin, to pay for it. Those sacrifices pointed to the death of Jesus, who offered himself as the final sacrifice. God prepared the nation of Israel through the sacrificial system for what Christ would do on the cross.

Here's how that truth plays out. Every week, our church, Redeemer Dubai, gathers people from around the world and all walks of life. It is not unusual for seventy nations to be represented in our service. It's a taste of heaven rarely known by the church on earth (Rev. 7:9).

I was preaching a series about how the Old Testament points to the gospel: from Joseph to Jonah to John the Baptist. One week, we were looking at the life of Abraham, specifically the Genesis 22 account in which God calls Abraham to sacrifice his beloved son Isaac. I mentioned how I had often heard this passage preached in the past: Abraham was a man of faith, and we need to be people of faith. Abraham was willing to sacrifice the most precious gifts in his life for God, and we need to be willing to sacrifice the most precious gifts in our lives for God. These are wonderful truths. But my concern is that if we leave it there, we miss the most important storyline of the passage.

Actually, when it comes to narrative passages of the Old Testament, it's usually a great mistake to put ourselves in the role of the hero—and that's certainly true here, because we're not Abraham (at least, I know I'm not). If we are anyone in this story, we are Isaac. Just like Isaac, we are bound—not by ropes, but by sin—and like Isaac, we are on the altar of God as his wrath hangs over us like a knife. Like Isaac, we have been condemned to death. Our only hope is that God will have mercy on us and spare us—and he does. He stops the sacrifice of our lives and provides another sacrifice. A ram was the substitute for Isaac, and Christ is our substitute. That's substitutionary atonement.

Certainly, Abraham was faithful, but the main point of the text is not how we can be more faithful, but how we need to understand the gospel in the provision of God for us. Genesis 22 is a foreshadowing of the gospel. This gospel theme starts in Genesis and continues throughout Scripture, so that when John the Baptist sees Jesus and says, "Behold, the Lamb of God, who takes away the sin of the world!" (John 1:29), everyone knows what he is talking about.

Substitutionary atonement: Christ died for me, in my place. For all who will repent and believe, their sins are paid for in full.

Just as substitutionary atonement comes from outside ourselves, so does imputed righteousness. But there is a distinction with imputation. Here's 2 Corinthians 5:21 again: "For our sake he made him to be sin who knew no sin, so that in him we might become the righteousness of God." Jesus never sinned, but he *became* sin. So when Paul says God made Jesus to be sin for us, he is telling us that God placed our sin on Jesus. Then God clothes all who repent and believe in Jesus with Christ's righteousness.

Imputed righteousness is another idea that is traced throughout Scripture, from its beginning in the first book of the Bible. My friend Mark Dever says that if there is one verse to circle in the Old Testament, it's Genesis 15:6, which tells us that Abraham "believed the Lord, and he counted it to him as righteousness."

Therefore, when we who are united with Christ stand before God in judgment (the judgment spoken of in 2 Cor. 5:10), God will declare us both forgiven because of substitutionary atonement and righteous because of imputed righteousness. I love John MacArthur's summary of the meaning of verse 21: "On the cross, God treated Christ as if He had committed all the sins of every sinner who would ever believe, so that He could treat every believer as if they had lived Christ's perfect life."[3]

How precious is this gospel message to you? When I explain substitutionary atonement or imputed righteousness, does your heart leap? Or are you more interested in the next meal? If this gospel doesn't bring great joy, well, you may not be a Christian.

Are you willing to give your life for the sake of the gospel? Are you willing to die? I suspect that many of you are. You're laying down your life for the hope of the gospel. In fact, your life does not make sense without the truth of the gospel. But here's a harder test: are you willing to call others to die for it?

Once, after I finished explaining substitutionary atonement and imputed righteousness at church, I saw Nisin leading a young man forward to me from the back.

"Mack, this is Mohammed, he wants to talk with you," Nisin said.

---

[3] John MacArthur, *MacArthur Study Bible* (Wheaton, IL: Crossway, 2010), note to 2 Cor. 5:21.

"Hello, Mohammed, good to meet you," I said.

Mohammed was eyeing my Bible. He asked, "Is that a Bible?"

"Yes," I said, wishing I had brought a cheaper Bible. "Would you like to have it?"

"Oh, I would very much," said Mohammed as he turned it over in his hands.

Then he added: "You know, I didn't know that about Abraham. I have never heard it. But my heart is drawn to it." He paused as he continued to look down at my Bible. "I'm from the Sudan, and if my father knew what I was thinking about, I think he would kill me."

I would be less than honest if I didn't admit that I felt that sharp tug at my heart: "Is it worth it? Is there some other way?" But I remembered something else, something I had to resolve long ago: it's better to know Jesus and live a short life than to not know Jesus and live a long life on earth, eking out what pleasure you might find before you die, and then meet Jesus in judgment without being clothed in his righteousness.

I believe Jesus is worth it.

Do you believe that? It's part of our call as ambassadors to make sure that we understand the preciousness of God's call in the gospel. If you do understand this, then you grasp what God has done in Christ. This understanding is essential to being an ambassador for Jesus.

In the end, Christ's ambassadors are motivated by the gospel; they see people with gospel eyes; they grasp the big story of God's gospel work in the world; they understand their role as ambassadors for the gospel; and they're grounded in the gospel truth of Christ's saving work in his death and resurrection.

May God make his appeal through us, for the spread of the gospel and the glory of Jesus Christ.

5

ARE PEOPLE WITHOUT CHRIST REALLY LOST?

Andrew Davis

In September 1865, Hudson Taylor stood trembling, gripping the side of the pulpit before a vast Christian assembly in Perth, Scotland. He was only thirty-three years old and just coming off his first missionary term in China. The words he was about to speak would come pouring from his heart and would be life changing for all who heard his message, a milestone in the history of missions. His goal was to shock his hearers out of lethargic indifference about missions. His method was to tell a true story about a Chinese man named Peter, whom Taylor had been trying to reach with the gospel.

Taylor and Peter had been traveling by junk along the coast of China, and at one point the man fell overboard (or perhaps jumped in—we'll never know). No one on the junk seemed to care much, but they did stop the junk so Taylor could make a frantic effort to try to bring Peter up. Suddenly, he spied some fishermen using a dragnet nearby—exactly what was needed at the moment. He called to the fishermen: "Come quickly! A man is drowning!"

Their response was stunning: "It's not convenient."

Taylor couldn't believe his ears. "Don't speak of convenience," he said. "Come quickly or it will be too late."

"We are busy fishing."

"Forget about your fishing; come, only come at once! I will pay you; I will pay you well."

"How much will you give us?"

"Five dollars. Only please don't stand there talking. Save life without delay."

"Too little. We will not come for less than thirty dollars."

"But I don't have that much with me," said Taylor. "I will give you everything I have."

"Well, how much is that?" they answered.

"Oh, I don't know . . . about fourteen dollars?"

With that, they decided to come. They passed their dragnet once over the place where the man had gone down and brought him up immediately. But it was too late—the man had died.

As Taylor told this story at that conference in Scotland, a kind of fiery indignation and revulsion came over the vast assembly. That is exactly what Taylor thought would happen, but then he drove the point home. "Is the body," he said, "of so much more value than the soul? We condemn those heathen fishermen. We say they were guilty of the man's death because they could easily have saved him. And they did not do it. But what of the millions whom we leave to perish? And that eternally! What of the plain command that God has given us: 'Go ye into all the world and preach the gospel to every creature?'"

Taylor then expanded on the value of a single soul to God and reported the mortality rate of thirty-three thousand who were dying daily without a Savior in China. He imagined the population of China (400 million) walking by him single file, one after the other, hour after hour, day after day, year after year. He said it would take twenty-three years for all of them to pass by. However, it would take the total number of converts at that time in China only a half hour to walk by. And, he said, with thirty-three thousand people perishing daily, in three months' time, the deaths would outnumber the population of London (approximately 3 million). Virtually all of those people were passing into eternity without hope and without God. This led to a phrase that came to be associated with Hudson Taylor: "A million a month dying without God." This controlling thought helped Taylor to make his urgent appeal for China, in Perth and everywhere he lectured.[1]

At the center of the passion that drove Taylor into a life of missionary service and into organizing the China Inland Mission is the question that stands in front of us right now: Are those without Christ lost? And even more pointed: What about those who die never having heard the gospel? There is before us a vast unfinished task, and we're aware of how daunting it is. The missions website joshuaproject.org says there are 16,594 unreached people groups. The world population is more than 7 billion, and 2.87 billion are in those unreached people groups; perhaps 3 billion or more have never heard the name of Christ at this time. Many others, of course, have heard his name but have not yet received him. How are we to understand the spiritual condition of those outside of Christ, and more specifically, those who have never heard the gospel? How are we to understand the character of God in all of this: his sovereignty in salvation, his justice in condemnation, his grace through Christ, his power in the Holy Spirit, and his wisdom in committing such a vital task to people such as us (who are so weak, changeful, rebellious, and indifferent)? How are we to understand and embrace our responsibility in all of this?

A Theological War Zone

As we come to these questions, we are sailing into a theological war zone,[2] and as we do, I will fly my flag right now: I am writing from

---

[1] Dr. and Mrs. Howard Taylor, *Hudson Taylor and the China Inland Mission—the Growth of a Work of God* (OMF International, 1998), 3–9.

[2] The following are resources for further study on this "theological war zone": William V. Crockett and James G. Sigountos, eds., *Through No Fault of Their Own: The Fate of Those Who Have Never Heard* (Grand Rapids: Baker, 1991); John Sanders, *No Other Name: An Investigation into the Destiny of the Unevangelized* (Grand Rapids: Eerdmans, 1992); Ronald Nash, *Is Jesus the Only Savior?* (Grand Rapids: Zondervan, 1994); John Sanders, ed., *What About Those Who Have Never Heard? Three Views on the Destiny of the Unevangelized* (Downers Grove, IL: InterVarsity, 1995); Dennis L. Okholm and Timothy R. Phillips, eds., *More Than One Way? Four Views on Salvation in a Pluralistic World* (Grand Rapids: Zondervan, 1995); Michael Green, *"But Don't All Religions Lead to God?" Navigating the Multi-Faith Maze* (Grand Rapids: Baker, 2002); Terrance L. Tiessen, *Who Can Be Saved? Reassessing Salvation in Christ and World Religions* (Downers Grove, IL: InterVarsity, 2004); Christopher W. Morgan and Robert A. Peterson, eds., *Faith Comes from Hearing: A Response*

a viewpoint commonly known as *exclusivism*. This viewpoint holds that only those who consciously place their faith in the Christ of the Bible are saved from sin, delivered from condemnation in hell. Beyond this, the view asserts that we have no biblical ground to expect that salvation to happen apart from human messengers taking the gospel to the ends of the earth. Contending against this view are a variety of others, including: (1) *universalism* (if there is a hell, it is empty of human beings); (2) *pluralism* (all religious faiths are equally valid ways of avoiding hell and making it to heaven); (3) *inclusivism* (conscious faith in Jesus Christ is not absolutely necessary for salvation—the sovereign God may use other means, including general revelation in creation, to save people); and (4) *accessibilism* (God is able to get the gospel content to the ends of the earth without using human messengers).

At this point in history, exclusivists take fire from people on every side of this issue. Universalists and pluralists consider the exclusive claims of Christianity to be arrogant; for us to assert that no one can be saved apart from faith in "our" Christ is offensive to their postmodern mindset and tolerance-loving ears. Others argue that there can be such a thing as anonymous Christians,[3] or maybe even better, unwitting Christians—people in other religions, such as Islam, Buddhism, and Hinduism, who are upright in the moral framework of their religion and are saved unwittingly through Christ; when they get to heaven, they will find out the full truth.

Some cite the example of Old Testament saints such as Melchizedek, to whom, it seems, God gave some kind of revelation or with whom he had some kind of relationship. They ask why God couldn't do that today. Others bring up the issue of infants who die or of special-needs adults who lack the mental capacity to understand

---

to Inclusivism (Downers Grove, IL: InterVarsity, 2008); Gerald R. McDermott, "Will All Be Saved?" *Themelios* 38, no. 2 (Summer 2013).

[3] Karl Rahner coined this term and defined an anonymous Christian as a "pagan . . . who lives in the state of Christ's grace through faith, hope, and love, yet who has no explicit knowledge of the fact that his life is oriented in grace-given salvation to Jesus Christ." (Karl Rahner, *Theological Investigations*, Vol. 14, trans. David Bourke [London: Darton, Longman, & Todd], 218). But the question that must be asked is this: How can anyone "believe in [someone] of whom they have never heard?" (Rom. 10:14). What is the "faith" of this "anonymous Christian," not to mention the true nature of his "hope and love"?

the gospel message,[4] asserting that these exceptional cases show there must be loopholes available. Some even argue for the possibility of a "second chance" for people to hear the gospel after death (though for many it would be the first chance).[5] Regarding the issue of who must spread the message, some say that God can use dreams or angels to preach the gospel to people at the ends of the earth.

Some Reformed thinkers say that it is arrogant for us to box in the sovereign God on this matter, so we ought to remain respectfully agnostic about the condition of those who have never heard the gospel—and just let God be God.

The Scriptures Compel an Answer

It is right for us to face these questions and address even the most complex challenges they pose. But as we do so, we should be confident that God has not left us in the dark, and that "everything we need for life and godliness" (2 Pet. 1:3) is found in a right reading of the Scriptures.[6] We do well to embrace and apply the sufficiency of Scripture to answer the pressing question of the destiny of those who have never heard the gospel.

And it is necessary and healthy for us to answer. While God can do awesome things through us even if we get the answer wrong, our missiology is hampered if we shrink back from facing this question or if we answer it wrongly. In the long term, it's best for us to face this question and address it biblically.

Six Key Assertions

Scripture does not speak with an uncertain voice on this issue; it needs no augmenting or editing. Jesus would rightly be able to point to clear biblical teachings and say to us, "How foolish you

---

[4] See note 12.

[5] Rob Bell is only the most recent influential advocate of this view in his *Love Wins: A Book about Heaven, Hell, and the Fate of Every Person Who Ever Lived* (New York: HarperCollins, 2011). Other recent advocates include George Lindbeck, Stephen Davis, and Gabriel Fackre.

[6] Unless otherwise indicated, Scripture references in this chapter are taken from The Holy Bible, New International Version®, NIV®. Copyright © 1973, 1978, 1984 by Biblica, Inc.™ Used by permission. All rights reserved worldwide.

are, and how slow of heart to believe all that the prophets have spoken!" (Luke 24:25). So we have to say with the psalmist, "Open my eyes that I may see wonderful things in your law" (Ps. 119:18). We must rely on Jesus to open our minds so that we can understand the Scriptures (Luke 24:45).

I would like to make six assertions relevant to this issue, and then discuss each one briefly based on Scripture: (1) those without Christ are lost; (2) there is no way for sinners to be saved apart from the shed blood of Christ; (3) there is no salvation apart from conscious faith in Christ; (4) the gospel must be proclaimed to the ends of the earth to bring about that conscious faith; (5) believers are responsible for that proclamation of the gospel; and (6) God is sovereign over the entire missions enterprise, guaranteeing its success.

Those without Christ Are Lost

Soon after I came to faith in Christ, I went to a "Q&A" session with John MacArthur, whose *Grace to You* radio broadcasts I heard daily. As soon as I saw that microphones had been set up, I stood in line to ask a question: "What about those who have never heard the gospel?" I'll never forgot how MacArthur began his answer: "You want to say they're okay, don't you? There is that instinct to say they're okay without Christ. But if they are okay, we need to leave them alone, because statistics show that whenever the gospel appears in some town, village, or city, it's generally rejected. Therefore, all the missionaries did was bring death and eternal destruction by going there to preach the gospel!" But the apostle Paul says in Romans 10:15: "As it is written, 'How beautiful are the feet of those who bring good news!'"

Scripture gives clear testimony to the spiritual state of those apart from Christ: they are lost. First John 5:19 says the whole world is under the control of the Evil One (Satan). Paul asserts that Satan, the "god of this age," has blinded the minds of unbelievers (2 Cor. 4:4), and that all of us were dead in our transgressions and sins, following Satan in rebellion against God (Eph. 2:1–3).

This is true all over the world, even in places where the truths of the Bible are completely unknown. Romans 1:20–21 says: "For since the creation of the world God's invisible qualities—his eternal power and divine nature—have been clearly seen, being understood from what has been made, so that people are without excuse. For although they knew God, they neither glorified him as God nor gave thanks to him, but their thinking became futile and their foolish hearts were darkened." A few verses later, Paul writes, "They exchanged the truth of God for a lie, and worshiped and served created things rather than the Creator—who is forever praised. Amen" (v. 25). All around the world, through his creation, God has left clear evidence of his existence and his nature: through sunrises and sunsets; mountains, canyons, and oceans; the birth of babies; the breaching of whales; the soaring of eagles; the roaring of lions. All creation testifies to a God of divine power, intricate wisdom, and gentle lovingkindness. For these reasons, Paul says people are without excuse, because they sin and they worship and serve created things rather than the Creator.

In Romans 2:14–15, Paul says that God has written his moral laws on people's hearts; their consciences alternately accuse and defend them. Those who live in the hearing of God's laws are guilty because they have the clear moral standards of God but fail to keep them (Rom. 2:17–24). Paul sums it all up in Romans 3:9–12 with his most potent language: "Jews and Gentiles alike are all under sin. As it is written: 'There is no one righteous, not even one; there is no one who understands, no one who seeks God. All have turned away, they have together become worthless; there is no one who does good, not even one.'"

Paul deepens this doctrine by revealing the mystery of our "original sin" in Adam. According to Romans 5:12–21, every single human being is born in Adam as a sinner, positionally, and every single person old enough to understand God's existence and moral law immediately sins in actuality, violating God's commandments. According to Romans 7:9, as soon as people understand God's laws, they turn away from him, suppressing the truth in unrighteousness, and they die spiritually by sinning against him. Without a Savior, they are powerless and have no hope whatsoever of finding refuge from the wrath to come. And their condemnation will be just, for God is perfectly just and righteous altogether. Romans 3:19 says every mouth will be silenced and the whole world held accountable to God. Without a Savior, someday they will hear these dreadful words: "Depart from me, you who are cursed, into the eternal fire prepared for the devil and his angels" (Matt. 25:41). Our inquiry into this topic must start with this biblical assertion: those without Christ are lost; they live every day under the coming wrath of God and cannot save themselves.

There Is No Salvation apart from the Shed Blood of Christ

Scripture makes plain that there is no way for sinners to be saved apart from the shed blood of Christ. Before we prove this assertion from Scripture, we who are believers in Christ ought to stop and simply celebrate. Praise God that there is a gospel at all! Praise God that he sent his Son into the world, not to condemn the world but to save it (John 3:17)! Praise God that Jesus came to seek and to save the lost (Luke 19:10)! Had God not crafted the salvation plan before the creation of the world and written it in the blood of his precious Son, there would be nothing for us to write about here, no topic to discuss—nothing but the fearful expectation of judgment and of raging fire that will consume the enemies of God (Heb. 10:27). We don't deserve this gospel, but thank God there is one!

But should we grieve that there aren't multiple ways to be saved? Just as there is one God and only one God, there is one gospel and only one gospel.

In our generation, the cultural air we breathe is fogged with postmodernism, tolerance, relativism, universalism, and inclusivism. Many cities in America and all over the world are vast melting pots, where people from various cultures and religions come together. People who live in such cities see the generosity, self-sacrifice, friendliness, and hospitality of neighbors and coworkers who are Muslims, Buddhists, Hindus, or adherents of other religions. As a result, it is easy to question the scriptural assertion that Jesus Christ is the only way of salvation. Sadly, some Christians start to breathe in that foggy air and wrongly get "humble" about Christianity; they backpedal, becoming unwilling to stand on the exclusivity of the gospel. Scripture alone can blow away this haze by the pure light of truth. The Bible makes it plain that sinners are saved only by the shed blood of Christ. This is the only plan for salvation.

The necessity of blood atonement was established even from the beginning, when God shed the blood of an animal to clothe the nakedness of Adam and Eve (Gen. 3:21). This was to establish the clear principle that God had already given Adam: all sin deserves the death penalty (Gen. 2:17; Rom. 6:23). The shedding of the blood of the animal represented the life of the victim being poured out in sacrifice before God, fulfilling the death penalty that sin deserved (Lev. 17:11). Throughout the Old Testament, the animal sacrificial system taught that all sin deserves the death penalty, that this penalty can be paid by a substitute, but that the substitute really can't be an animal. "Without the shedding of blood there is no forgiveness" (Heb. 9:22), but "It is impossible for the blood of bulls and goats to take away sins" (Heb. 10:4).

Jesus Christ is the fulfillment of the animal sacrificial system, shedding his blood as a substitute for our sins. John the Baptist pointed to him and said, "Look, the Lamb of God, who takes away the sin of the world!" (John 1:29). Note that Jesus takes away the sin *of the world*! He is not merely a Jewish Savior. By faith in his blood, God's wrath is propitiated and sinners are justified (forgiven), no longer held accountable for all their sins (Rom. 3:25). Revelation 5:9 shows the heavenly celebration for the achievement of Christ: "And they sang a new song: 'You are worthy to take the scroll and to open its seals, because you were slain, and with your blood you purchased men for God from every tribe and language and people and nation.'" The blood of Christ is a sure and certain ground for forgiveness of sins by almighty God.

But the question in front of us is this: Is the shed blood of Christ *the only way* for sinners to be saved? For many people, this question is of passionate interest at many levels. But not one person on the earth asks this question with greater intensity than Jesus Christ asked it at Gethsemane. As hymn writer Joseph Hart put it, "View him groveling in the Garden,"[7] with sweat pouring out and great drops of blood falling to the earth. Hear him with immeasurable intensity praying this prayer: "My Father, *if it is possible*, may this cup be taken from me. Yet not as I will, but as you will" (Matt. 26:39). The answer must have come back so clearly from his loving Father: "No, my Son, *there is no other way*. You must shed your blood; you must drink this cup." And so, a second time he prayed, "My Father, if it is not possible for this cup to be taken away unless I drink it, may your will be done" (Matt. 26:42). That should settle this question forever. There was no other way than that Jesus should shed his blood; thus, there is no other way for people to be saved than by the blood of Jesus.

When, a few moments later, Peter tried to rescue Jesus from arrest, Jesus told him to put his sword away, saying: "How then would the Scriptures be fulfilled that say it must happen in this way?" (Matt. 26:54). There is no other way! This is the same assertion Jesus made that same night: "I am the way and the truth and the life. No one comes to the Father except through me" (John 14:6). No person on the earth will enter heaven and live eternally in the presence of God the Father apart from the saving work of Christ.

Other New Testament writers pick up this theme and state it explicitly. As Peter and John were on trial before the Jewish council for an act of kindness shown to a cripple, they were asked how he was healed. Peter, filled with the Holy Spirit, stood and testified with tremendous boldness to the exclusivity of the gospel: "It is by the name of Jesus Christ of Nazareth, whom you crucified but whom God raised from the dead, that this man stands before you

---

[7] From the hymn "Come, Ye Sinners, Poor and Needy" by Joseph Hart, 1759.

healed. He is 'the stone you builders rejected, which has become the capstone.' Salvation is found in no one else, for there is no other name under heaven given to men by which we must be saved" (Acts 4:10–12).

I believe that this is the strongest exclusivist passage in the Bible. Look at the geographical scope of the statement: there is "no other name *under heaven.*" There's not a square inch of land on this globe where it is not true that Christ is the only Savior. Look at the ethnic scope: "no other name *given to men*"; it's not given just to Jews, but to all humanity. Look at the christological scope: it's by the name of Jesus Christ of Nazareth that we are saved. That name involves a biography; it involves the person and work of Christ being communicated. Look at the absolute necessity of the language here: salvation is found in *no one* else. And then, at the end, hear the words "by which we *must* be saved." It is necessary for us to be saved this way. This passage testifies eloquently that there is no other Savior, no other salvation.

Another verse worthy of consideration is Galatians 2:21. Paul says, "I do not set aside the grace of God, for if righteousness could be gained through the law, Christ died for nothing!" The most common attempts at self-salvation involve moralism—keeping "the law." Paul says such attempts are proven to be impossible by the very fact of Christ's life and death. Our heavenly Father did not send his only begotten Son into the world to provide one of many ways to get to heaven. He sent him to provide *the* way to be saved.

There Is No Salvation apart from Conscious Faith in Christ

Here I want to appeal to two steps I learned from John Murray in his classic book *Redemption Accomplished and Applied.*[8] Redemption was accomplished once for all by the shed blood of Christ,[9] but then the blood had to be applied. At the first Passover, the lamb was slaughtered and its blood poured out, and then that blood was

---

[8] John Murray, *Redemption Accomplished and Applied* (Grand Rapids: Eerdmans, 1985).
[9] See Romans 3:24; also Hebrews 7:27; 9:12, 26, 28; 10:10.

applied to the doorposts and the lintels with the branches of a hyssop plant (Ex. 12:22). So also the redemption that Christ worked at the cross has to be applied—by the Holy Spirit to individual sinners through faith.

Paul makes this application of the blood to individual sinners very explicit. Having established the universality of sin in Romans 1–3, Paul sums it all up: "For all have sinned and fall short of the glory of God, and are justified by his grace as a gift, through the redemption that is in Christ Jesus, whom God put forward as a propitiation by his blood, *to be received by faith*" (Rom. 3:23–25 ESV). God presented Jesus Christ as a propitiation (a sacrifice that turns away the wrath of God) by his blood. This is redemption accomplished. But this propitiation is received by faith. This is redemption applied. Only through faith in the blood of Christ can we be justified, receive forgiveness of sins, and receive the imputed righteousness of Christ.

In Galatians 2:11–17, Paul tells how he rebuked Peter for behaving hypocritically, drawing back from Gentile converts as though they were second-class citizens. The false teachers were saying the Gentiles couldn't be justified unless they kept the law of Moses, and Peter was intimidated by them and acted wrongly. Therefore, Paul had to address that sin to Peter's face: "We . . . know that a man is not justified by observing the law, but *by faith in Jesus Christ*. So we, too, have put our *faith in Christ Jesus* that we may be justified by *faith in Christ* and not by observing the law, because by observing the law no one will be justified. . . . We . . . seek to be justified *in Christ*." Four times in three verses Paul affirms that it is only by faith in Christ Jesus (or Jesus Christ) that a sinner is justified. It couldn't be plainer. So it is not enough to be what some call "a person of faith." We have to have faith *in Jesus Christ*.

What, then, of the Old Testament saints such as Melchizedek? In every era of redemptive history, men and women must respond with faith and obedience to the revelation that God has graciously granted up to that point. We are always obligated to trust God and his Word. But we must also say that with the coming of Christ, that era of redemptive history is over. As Paul said to the philosophers of Athens, "The times of ignorance God overlooked, but now he commands all people everywhere to repent" (Acts 17:30 ESV). There is now no salvation apart from conscious faith in Jesus Christ.

There Is No Conscious Faith apart from Verbal Proclamation of the Gospel

It is impossible for anyone to come to conscious faith in Jesus Christ without the verbal proclamation of the gospel. For this reason, this gospel must be proclaimed to the ends of the earth. Here we come to the inexorable logic of Romans 10:13–15: "'Everyone who calls on the name of the Lord will be saved.' How, then, can they call on the one they have not believed in? And how can they believe in the one of whom they have not heard? And how can they hear without someone preaching to them? And how can they preach unless they are sent? As it is written, 'How beautiful are the feet of those who bring good news!'" This passage, I think, is the strongest argument for the necessity of missions in the Bible. It is an unbreakable chain of rhetorical questions, all of which assume the same answer: *no.* Can anyone call on someone he doesn't believe in? *No.* Can anyone believe in someone of whom he has never heard? *No.* Can anyone hear something without someone telling him? *No.* Can anyone tell him without being sent? *No.*

Let's push it even further—let's go to the language of impossibility. Paul's assumptions here are astonishing. Paul clearly assumes it is impossible for anyone to be saved without calling on the name of the Lord Jesus. This rules out universalism and pluralism. And it is impossible for anyone to call on Jesus without first believing in him with a heart of faith. Faith must precede any true "sinner's prayer." This rules out inclusivism. And it is impossible for anyone to believe in Jesus without first hearing of him. That is the key step in the assertion we're making here. It's impossible to have justifying faith without first hearing of Jesus Christ. This rules out accessibilism.

This means that knowledge of the facts of the gospel is essential to salvation. You have to get the biography of Jesus uploaded in your mind in a way you can understand. You have to hear of Jesus of Nazareth, Son of God, Son of Man, born of a virgin, leading a sinless life, doing miracles, and dying on the cross. You have to hear the significance of the substitutionary atonement. You have to hear of his bodily resurrection and of the need for repentance and faith.

Paul's final step in the chain has been the dynamo for twenty centuries of world missions: it is impossible to hear of Christ without someone being sent to preach. The clear assumption here is that *human* messengers have to be sent. The awesome glories of God in creation (sunrises, sunsets, soaring eagles, newborn babies, and many more), however marvelously they testify to the existence of a Creator God, do not tell us of his Son and his saving work on the cross. That message must be proclaimed, and those who proclaim it must be sent out. As Paul says in Romans 10:17, "Faith comes from hearing the message, and the message is heard through the word of Christ." The proclamation of this gospel message is the end purpose of this chapter and, indeed, of the entire missionary drive of the church. It is the central story of the last twenty centuries of human history, from the heavenly perspective. For the sake of this gospel message, the church must renew its zeal for missions in every generation, even day after day. The church must heed the unbreakable chain of Romans 10:13–15 that comes down from heaven with convicting fire, with weighty obligation, with compelling purpose, and with delightful reward.

Believers Are Responsible to Proclaim the Gospel

This proclamation of the gospel is our responsibility—it has been committed to *us*. At the end of each Gospel, there is a version of the Great Commission, given from the lips of the resurrected Lord Jesus himself to his disciples and, by implication, to us as well. The most famous, of course, is Matthew 28:19–20, where Christ commissions his disciples to make disciples of all nations. In Mark

16:15–16, the command is to go into all creation and preach the gospel; whoever believes and is baptized will be saved, but whoever does not believe will be condemned. In Luke 24:47–48, Jesus couples a prophecy, "repentance and forgiveness of sins will be preached . . . to all nations, beginning in Jerusalem," with an assertion that functions as a command: "You are witnesses of these things." In John 20:21, Jesus says, "As the Father has sent me, I am sending you." Then come his beautiful words in Acts 1:8: "You will receive power when the Holy Spirit comes on you; and you will be my witnesses in Jerusalem, and in all Judea and Samaria, and to the ends of the earth." So we are responsible because Christ has commanded us to do this.

This command was the driving theme of Paul's life. He considered his life worth nothing to him except to testify to the nations of the gospel of God's grace (Acts 20:24). Paul says God has committed to us the ministry of reconciliation and sent us out as ambassadors, as though God himself were making his appeal through us (2 Cor. 5:19–20). Paul says he was not "disobedient to the vision from heaven" (Acts 26:19); he would have considered failure to preach the gospel to be rebellion against Jesus. He was especially ambitious to take the gospel to those who had never heard it (Rom. 15:20).

What, then, are our responsibilities to those who have never heard the gospel? First, we should respond with *passion*. The plight of the perishing should matter to us, as it clearly did to Hudson Taylor and to the apostle Paul. In Romans 9:2, Paul says, "I have great sorrow and unceasing anguish in my heart" for the lost among the Jews. William Carey, the father of modern missions, was similarly passionate. When he was an apprentice shoemaker, he made a globe out of shoe leather on which he depicted the nations, and, with tears running down his face, he would say, "These are all heathen!"[10] We must respond with this kind of passion.

We should also respond with *prayer*: "Brothers, my heart's de-

---

[10] Quoted in S. Pearce Carey, *William Carey* (London: Hodder and Stoughton, 1923), 51.

sire and prayer to God for the Israelites is that they may be saved" (Rom. 10:1). Paul frequently solicited prayer support for his missionary work. He says in 2 Thessalonians 3:1, "Finally, brothers, pray for us that the message of the Lord may spread rapidly and be honored, just as it was with you." In other words, Paul wants the Thessalonians to pray that he and his team might preach the gospel effectively among unbelievers, and that people might hear and respond in belief, rapidly. He is yearning for prayer. So we should pray for missions and missionaries.

We should respond with *planning*. We should use carefully considered means for the conversion of the heathen. Carey put it right in the title of his history-making tract in 1792: *An Enquiry into the Obligations of Christians to Use Means for the Conversion of the Heathens.* He was arguing against some extremists, who were saying that because God is sovereign, we do not need to do anything. No! We have an obligation to use means. We've got to plan and hold conferences, draw together, and strategize to figure out the best way to reach this group or that group.

Then comes the hard part: we should respond with *proclamation*, laying down our lives sacrificially and in willingness to suffer to make the plans born from passion and saturated in prayer come true, as we proclaim the gospel. Paul says in Colossians 1:24, "Now I rejoice in what was suffered for you, and I fill up in my flesh what is still lacking in regard to Christ's afflictions, for the sake of his body, which is the church." We should not understand that statement as any denigration of the atonement of Christ. Redemption has been accomplished once and for all; nothing can be added. "It is finished!" Jesus cried. But now it needs to be applied, and that can happen only by means of the suffering of evangelists and missionaries. Paul in effect says, "I rejoice in the suffering, and I am filling up some of that myself to take the gospel to the next step."

What about you, dear reader? Are you passionate about this gospel? Has this discussion of it kindled your affection? Pray to God that your affection and passion for the gospel would grow deeper. Are you praying for the lost and for the unreached people groups? Pray that God would give you deeper, more fervent, and more knowledgeable prayers. Are you making plans; are you involved in strategizing to reach the unreached people groups? Pray that God would give you a strategy, a plan, an angle, or something that could be a means to reaching the heathen, as Carey would put it. Are you in the process of laying down your life or sacrificially giving of your time, of your body, and of your future by going on short-term missions or career missions? What is the call of God on you and on your life? Could it be that God is calling you right now to this kind of ministry? Are you willing to suffer and to make sacrifices for the cause of world missions?

We cannot count on angels to do it. They would do an incredible job, no doubt. They could look very much like human beings; they wouldn't have to dress in their glorious garb and they wouldn't have to shock people. Scripture says people have entertained angels without knowing it (Heb. 13:2). They would be utterly fearless. We know that they were there at the birth of Christ and that they announced his birth to the shepherds. They were there at the resurrection and they announced it to the women: "He is not here; he has risen" (Matt. 28:6). So angels are capable of taking the gospel anywhere in the world.

However, two incidents in the book of Acts indicate that the job of gospel proclamation is not given to angels. In Acts 8, an angel tells Philip to go down to a desert road, where eventually he is going to preach to an Ethiopian eunuch. The angel does not go preach to the Ethiopian eunuch; the angel sends Philip to do it. Then, in Acts 10–11, an angel appears to Cornelius, a Roman centurion. The angel says: "Send to Joppa for Simon who is called Peter. He will bring you a message through which you and all your household will be saved" (11:13–14). So it seems that the angels refrain from actually preaching. I would simply put it this way: we have no biblical reason to expect God to send angels to preach the gospel. And the idea that angels are capable of preaching the gospel should in no way lessen the urgency of Romans 10:13–15 or the necessity of obedience concerning Christ's various missionary commissions to each of us.

God Is Sovereign over Missions, Guaranteeing Success

I have always been a little uncomfortable with appeals about "thousands dying every day," similar to the one made by Hudson Taylor that I recounted at the beginning of this chapter. There is a biblical theme of passionate urgency that is right and Christlike, but not a tone of faithless panic, as if the whole missions enterprise might fail if we don't act immediately. I want to establish all missional appeals on the biblically solid ground of this assertion: God is absolutely sovereign over the whole process.

While Romans 10:13–15 gives an unbreakable chain leading to vigorous missionary activity, so Romans 8:28–30 gives an unbreakable chain of God's sovereign activity in the life of every elect person: "And we know that in all things God works for the good of those who love him, who have been called according to his purpose. For those God foreknew he also predestined to be conformed to the likeness of his Son, that he might be the firstborn among many brothers. And those he predestined, he also called; those he called, he also justified; those he justified, he also glorified."

Follow this unbreakable logic based on God's sovereignty. God is actively working for the eternal good for every person "called according to his purpose." That "purpose" is election resulting in the final glorification of individual sinners. God is powerfully working out his wise and complex plan in the life of every single elect person.

The "unbreakable chain" in verses 28–30 follows specific people God has in mind—those he "predestined" (v. 29). Ephesians 1:4–5 tells us God elected and predestined his people before the foundation of the world. According to Romans 8:28–30, God foreknows specific people, meaning he sets his covenant love on them, not merely that he "knows about them" or knows ahead of time what

they will do.[11] Every predestined person gets a call, which biblically means a clear proclamation of the gospel coupled with an
effective working by the Holy Spirit in his/her heart to repent and
believe. *That means not a single elect person will fail to hear the
gospel!*[12] That is a huge assertion for this topic, but it can be received only by faith based on sound exegesis.

Next in the unbreakable chain, every single elect person God
calls, he also justifies. And every single elect person God justifies,
he also glorifies. Not a single person "slips through the cracks."
God's sovereign power guarantees success in every case!

So the missionary enterprise is a hunt for the elect. The problem
is that they do not have an "E" on their foreheads, as we certainly
have noticed! We're told to preach to everyone, to "all creation"
(Mark 16:15). Many are "called" in that sense, by hearing the general invitation, but only a few are chosen (Matt. 22:14). The greatest
missionary in church history, the apostle Paul, says in 2 Timothy
2:10, "I endure everything *for the sake of the elect,* that they too
may obtain the salvation that is in Christ Jesus, with eternal glory."
He did it all for the elect, and no one poured himself out for missions with more determination and suffering than Paul. The only

---

[11] On judgment day, Jesus will say to some people: "I never *knew* you! Away from me, you evildoers!" (Matt.
7:23). This shows clearly that Jesus is not referring to "knowing about" someone, for he knows *everything*
about them! He knows that they are "evildoers." Matthew 12:36 says sinners will have to give an account
for "every careless word they have spoken." So Jesus, the Judge of all the earth, "knows about" these people
with perfect and comprehensive knowledge. But he will still be able to say he never knew *them.* This is
electing, covenant love, as in a marriage. Genesis 4:1 says, "Adam knew his wife Eve; and she conceived; and
bare Cain" (KJV). Mary said to Gabriel concerning the baby Jesus who would be formed in her womb, "How
shall this be, seeing I know not a man?" (Luke 1:34 KJV). She knew lots of men, but she was not intimate
with any. So also God "foreknows" sinners personally; he covenants with them in his mind before the foundation of the world and determines by sovereign grace to do them good. This is what Paul means when he
writes, "Those God foreknew he also predestined" (Rom. 8:29). Predestination is not based on foreseen faith.
[12] I do not desire to go into details here on the issue of infants who die in infancy or of special-needs adults
who cannot understand the gospel in the ordinary way. This assertion is made with the understanding that
we're talking about ordinary people who grow to adulthood. I believe (as many others do) that infants who
die in infancy are all elect, but their salvation is different from that of others because their sin is different
from that of others. They only sin in Adam, hence their death (Rom. 5:12–14). But they do not sin as Adam
did by breaking a command. So just as God applied the sin of Adam to them apart from their understanding, he applies the redemption of Christ to them apart from their understanding. My central ground for
this assertion comes from Romans 5:12–14 (as noted), Romans 7:9, and also all the biblical depictions of
judgment day, in which people are judged by what they have done, as recorded in God's books (Rev. 20:12;
cf. Rom. 2:6). I am aware others reject this and can embrace a doctrine of infant damnation, while others say
we should remain silent on these speculative topics. But I think the verses cited give enough insight to go
as far as I've gone. So I believe that Romans 8:28–30 teaches that all the elect who reach normal adulthood
will hear a clear presentation of the gospel.

way, though, that we can know who the elect are is through their response to the gospel. Paul writes in 1 Thessalonians 1:4, "For we know, brothers loved by God, that he has chosen you." In other words, Thessalonians, we know you're elect. How? "Because our gospel came to you not simply with words, but also with power, with the Holy Spirit and with deep conviction" (v. 5). Their response to the gospel was proof of their eternal election—it had roots in the mind of God before the foundation of the world.

God is sovereign also in giving the gospel message to whom he chooses. He doesn't owe the gospel to any sinner, for he doesn't owe anything to anyone. "Who has ever given to God, that God should repay him?" (Rom. 11:35). That concept should make every Christian eternally grateful to God, for we heard the gospel even though we didn't deserve to hear it. God is sovereign also to get that gospel message to any place he chooses on the face of the earth. No place is too far for God, though it might seem very remote to us. God's arm is not too short to save. He sits enthroned above the circle of the earth, and its people all look like grasshoppers to him (Isa. 40:22). The nations are like a drop from the bucket and dust on the scales (v. 15). Is there any remote island in the South Pacific or secluded valley in the Andes Mountains that God cannot reach with the gospel? No.

In 1947, Norwegian ethnologist and adventurer Thor Heyerdahl proved his theory that the islands of the South Pacific, some of the most remote inhabited places on the face of the earth, were peopled from the coastlands of South America by simple rafts that followed the currents in the Pacific Ocean. In the famous *Kon-Tiki* expedition, he traveled by a hand-made raft over 4,300 nautical miles from South America to the Tuamotu Islands in the South Pacific. The voyage took 101 days.[13] If he could do that by such primitive means, why couldn't God deliver the gospel in a short time anywhere on the planet by human messengers? We should not assume that church history is a perfect and complete record. We

---

[13] Thor Heyerdahl, *Kon-Tiki: Across the Pacific by Raft*, trans. F. H. Lyon (New York: Rand McNally, 1960), 1–10.

don't know that God didn't deliver the gospel to some elect people in some nation in the thirteenth century just because we have no record of it. God is able to get the gospel anywhere he wants, anytime he wants. He doesn't need to send angels; he can send human messengers and keep the elect alive until his messengers get there.

And should we not praise him for the astonishing progress the gospel is making, even before our very eyes? Over the last century, there has been an amazing acceleration of missionary advance, to the eternal glory of God. As Paul says in Romans 10:18, "Their voice has gone out into all the earth, their words to the ends of the world." And again, in Romans 15:23, "There is no more place for me to work in these regions." What was true in the Mediterranean world in Paul's time is happening today on a global scale. The gospel is spreading faster and faster, and God is sovereignly raising up laborers for the harvest field and compelling them to go, putting a burden on their hearts so compelling they can't shake it off.

And so, we have this compulsion of the Spirit, as Paul says: "And now, *compelled* by the Spirit, I am going to Jerusalem, not knowing what will happen to me there. I only know that in every city the Holy Spirit warns me that prison and hardships are facing me" (Acts 20:22–23); "When I preach the gospel, I cannot boast, for I am *compelled* to preach. Woe to me if I do not preach the gospel!" (1 Cor. 9:16); and again, "Christ's love *compels* us" (2 Cor. 5:14). There's a constraining force on the heart of the individual, and the Holy Spirit can give it to any of his chosen workers any time he wills.

Not only does the Spirit compel the workers to go out, he also tells them specifically where to go. When Paul and Silas were on their missionary journey, they were blocked by the Spirit from going east to Asia (Acts 16:6). Then the Macedonian call came, and they went west, to Europe (vv. 9–10). The Spirit was orchestrating the direction.

God is also sovereign in working "both sides of the equation," both getting missionaries ready to go and preparing lost people to hear. It is beautiful how, in Acts 10, God works in Cornelius to get him ready to hear; works in Peter to get him ready to preach; and then brings them together. Ephesians 2:10 says, "For we are God's workmanship, created in Christ Jesus to do good works, which God *prepared in advance* for us to do." God is preparing elect people now to hear missionaries, and he is sovereign to keep those people alive until the missionaries get there. God is sovereign, therefore, in delivering the gospel to every elect person before he or she dies— every single one. Not a single elect person will be lost.

Because this is true, we ought to speak with the same joyous confidence that we see in many biblical texts that address the absolute certainty of the spread of the gospel to the ends of the earth. Take Psalm 22, for example, the great crucifixion psalm that begins, "My God, my God, why have you forsaken me?" and which clearly predicts the piercing of Christ's hands and feet (v. 16). Those details were foretold and therefore were absolutely certain. So also is the spread of the gospel. Listen to the words of Psalm 22:27–31:

> All the ends of the earth
> > *will* remember and turn to the LORD,
> and all the families of the nations
> > *will* bow down before him,
> for *dominion* belongs to the LORD,
> > and he *rules* over the nations.
> All the rich of the earth *will* feast and worship;
> > all who go down to the dust *will* kneel before him—
> > those who cannot keep themselves alive.
> Posterity *will* serve him;
> > future generations *will* be told about the Lord.
> They *will* proclaim his righteousness
> > to a people yet unborn—
> > for *he has done it.*

Feel the sense of certainty. If you go out as a missionary, and if you give your life in service to Christ, even if you're martyred, when you get to heaven, you will give Christ all the glory for what you did. God will do works in you by his sovereign grace, and they're going to happen. As Jesus said with unequivocal certainty, "This gospel of the kingdom will be preached in the whole world as a testimony to all nations, and then the end will come" (Matt. 24:14).

A settled assurance of the final victory of God over the world, the flesh, and the Devil, resulting in every single elect person being saved, should buoy all our thinking and actions in missions. So away with pathos-filled, man-centered missionary appeals that reek of failure and frantic pessimism! Instead, whenever we call on people to sacrifice for the unreached peoples of the world, let us do so with an open display of confidence that the sovereignty of God guarantees complete success. Our "labor in the Lord is not in vain!" (1 Cor. 15:58).

6

THE INDIVIDUAL'S SUFFERING AND THE SALVATION OF THE WORLD

Michael Oh

In April 2005, just ten days after the opening of Christ Bible Seminary in Nagoya, Japan, my wife Pearl and I were called to a hospital in Japan to get the results of our second daughter Mikaela's head MRI. We were thankful to hear that there were no problems with the virus and seizures that she had had, but then the doctors told us, "Your daughter has a brain tumor." That was the worst day of my life.

It seems that no matter how much we want to or how hard we try, we can't avoid suffering. And invariably, when we suffer, we ask questions:

- Why?
- Is God really good?
- Does God really love me?

Psalm 22 answers some of these questions, showing us that God does have a purpose for suffering in our lives—and that the blessings of that suffering are not just for us, but for people all around the world.

So here's the main theme for this chapter:

God has been, is, and will be faithful to his people, both corporately and individually, in suffering, and through such suffering all the nations will worship him as he is proclaimed by his suffering people.

This psalm has two distinct parts: prayer (vv. 1–21) and proclamation (vv. 22–31).

Prayer (vv. 1–21)

One way we can look at the first section of Psalm 22 is to see the painful and perplexing contrasts in David's mind in the midst of his suffering. First, in verses 1 and 2, we see the contrast between David's cries and God's silence:

> My God, my God, why have you forsaken me?
>> Why are you so far from saving me, from the words of
>> my groaning?
> O my God, I cry by day, but you do not answer,
>> and by night, but I find no rest.

David here is complaining about the perceived distance and silence of "his" God.

When I was a child, my mother accidentally spilled hot soup on my leg. I clearly remember crying and crying. To be honest, I also remember another thing—that it didn't really hurt that much. I think the reason why I cried so much was that the soup was spilled by my mom! My pain, however little it was, was caused by my own mother.

In verse 1, we can hear pain in David's voice—not because he feels forsaken by just *any* God, but by "*my* God, *my* God."

A second contrast we can see in David's words is that between God's faithfulness to Israel and God's forsaking of him. In verses 3–5, David is proclaiming or even reminding God of God's faithfulness to his people in the past. Throughout history, God has responded to the suffering and cries of his people; David knows this, and he brings it up with God. His prayer, his honest complaint to God, is:

> When Israel trusted in you, you saved them;
>> when I trust in you, why do you not save me?
> When Israel cried to you, you rescued them;
>> when I cry to you, why do you not rescue me?

There is a painful disconnect between what David knows of who God is and what God has done in the past—*and* what God is not doing for David now.

We see a third contrast in verses 12–18: David's enemies are near, but God is far from him. David characterizes his enemies as animals of prey that surround him. Because we've probably never been on the same side of a cage as a tiger, we don't understand how dangerous such a beast can be. A few years ago, a young girl named Haley Hilderbrand was having her high school graduation picture taken with a tiger—a school tradition.[1] She heard something and let out a squeal. Panicking, she started to run—just moments before the tiger lunged at her and killed her. Like that tiger, David's fierce enemies are near—too near. In verses 12–13, David cries that they encompass him, surround him, and threaten to tear him apart with their sharp teeth. In verse 16, he says they encompass him, encircle him, and pierce his hands and feet.

David's enemies are so near, but God seems so far away. Imagine if that teenage girl were crying out to her father as the tiger pounced upon her, but her father just looked on from a distance. That's how David felt.

This section of the psalm ends in verses 19–21 with David giving a final gasp and cry to God before being overwhelmed: "O Lord, do not be far off! . . . Come quickly. . . . Deliver my soul. . . . Save me!"

And then it's as if the curtain falls to end the first act of this

---

[1] The Associated Press, "Tiger kills Kansas teen posing for photo," August 19, 2005, http://www.nbcnews.com/id/9005475/ns/us_news-life/t/tiger-kills-kansas-teen-posing-photo/#.UzQm-qhdWa8 (accessed March 26, 2014).

drama. There is such a clear break in the psalm that some scholars have wrongly thought the two parts must be two different psalms. What brought about this tremendous shift in tone? We don't know. David doesn't tell us. It's almost as if Act Two of this drama were missing and we skip immediately to Act Three.

Although we do not know exactly what David experienced that resulted in the shift from verse 21 to verse 22, from our own experience in the midst of suffering, as well as from a broader biblical context, let me suggest three things that David learned and that we all can learn in the midst of suffering. After we consider these three points, we'll examine the second section of the psalm.

1. God Is in Control—of Everything

The first temptation, when suffering comes, is to think, "Maybe God isn't in control." But nowhere in this psalm do we see any indication that David sees himself as a victim of random fate. David is clearly giving God all the credit and blame for his circumstances.

The biblical reality is that God is sovereignly working out all that he has sovereignly ordained from eternity past, both in the world and in our lives, including our salvation and our sanctification—a very big part of which often includes suffering. And that's a very good thing, because . . .

2. Suffering Is a Part of the Good Design of God

The second temptation, when suffering comes, is to think, "If God's in control and I'm suffering like this, maybe God isn't good or maybe his plans aren't good."

So why is suffering good and also a part of God's good plan? First, let me suggest that suffering was designed for non-Christians—a very strange comment to make! If you are not yet a Christian today, I want to suggest to you that suffering functions to teach you of your need for Jesus Christ.

Let me introduce you to a little boy named Roberto Salazar,

whom you might initially envy.[2] Roberto feels no pain; as a baby, he never cried because of being hungry, tired, hurt, or in discomfort from a wet diaper, for he felt no pain. Roberto is one of seventeen people in the United States with "congenital insensitivity to pain with anhidrosis." It might sound like a dream condition to have no pain, but, as his parents say, it's really a nightmare. For instance, he never felt hunger pain, so he didn't eat. Likewise, when he started teething, he gnawed on his own tongue, lips, and fingers to the point of mutilation.

Pain is a God-given indicator that something is wrong. So the pain that you feel in your life as a whole is God's message to you that something is wrong, and the most significant thing that's wrong is the broken relationship with the God who made you.

I serve as a missionary in Japan and founded a ministry called CBI (Christian Bible Institute) Japan. Modernist sentiment would tell us that Japan, as one of the most technologically advanced societies in the world, should be one of the least pain-troubled nations of the world. The biblical perspective, however, affirms and informs the reality that Japan, as the largest unreached nation in the world, is filled to overflowing with humanly insolvable pain.

Why do 9 percent of high school girls sell their bodies to dirty old businessmen? Because they need $300? No! They already have money; they spend the $300 on something like a Gucci wallet the next day.

Why do 4 percent of middle school girls sell their bodies to dirty old businessmen? Because of pain—pain from spiritual emptiness accentuated and aggravated by the pains of life in a fallen world, including absent fathers working ninety-hour weeks, 60 percent of whom have paid for sex with prostitutes, possibly even their own daughters' classmates.

Do you think that the wealth of the Japanese makes them more happy? If we allow wealth to be our source of trust, pride, and com-

---

[2] Chris Gajilan, "World without pain is hell, parent says," September 28, 2006, CNN International, http://edition.cnn.com/2006/HEALTH/conditions/01/27/rare.conditions/index.html?section=cnn_latest (accessed March 26, 2014).

fort, sooner or later we learn that wealth can create *more* emptiness, *more* empty promises, and *more* empty hearts. The rich are not to be envied! Those who love their riches are to be pitied.

Now, of course, poverty and hunger are not blessings in and of themselves, but poverty can be a blessing because it can strengthen and heighten our understanding of the reality of our need for God. Blessed are those who know their emptiness, their need—their hunger.

But whether for the physically poor of the world—or, as in Japan, the spiritually poor—Christians must be there to help point out the lessons of pain and to point to the solution to pain in Christ.

Five years ago, the Lord gave our team at CBI Japan a vision to see the gospel of Jesus Christ shine in the very heart of the city of Nagoya: the place where much of the teenage prostitution of Japan occurs, where kids are being bullied and many resort to suicide, where hopeless young people gather to be hopeless together. Our vision was to establish a safe place for young people in the heart of the city—a place where young people could be physically, emotionally, relationally, sexually, and spiritually safe in the gospel!

Honestly, there were moments when we had to ask ourselves why God would give us a vision for something that seemed as if it could never become a reality—at least financially. Japanese real estate is infamously expensive. During the real estate bubble, which burst about twenty years ago, a 5-by-7-foot plot of land in downtown Nagoya cost about $130,000. But we continued to pray, wait, and believe that God would open a door for ministry in the heart of Nagoya.

Finally, suddenly, a door opened. We discovered a property that was strategically located in the city. Its value during the real estate bubble was more than $8 million, but the sale price was about $1.3 million. That was a huge bargain—but still about $1.2 million more than I had ever raised!

So we called for ninety days of prayer, and people all around the world began to pray—and to give! Missionaries around the world—from America, China, and even Afghanistan—gave a total of $50,000. By the amazing grace of God and the help of friends, churches, missionaries around the world, and complete strangers, by day eighty-two we had received $1.3 million.

It was a mighty act of God! But after we reached 100 percent of our goal, the property was gone. We were one week too late.

The very next week, however, we heard about another property, a larger building on a larger piece of land at a better location— just a five-minute walk from Nagoya Station! We thought it would surely cost $5 million; during the real estate bubble, the property was probably worth close to $20 million. But by God's grace, in 2011 we received the keys to that property for $1.2 million.

Today, in addition to Christ Bible Seminary, our first floor is home to the Heart & Soul Café—the fulfillment of that vision for a safe space. God miraculously provided for us so that we could have a presence with those who are in pain, with those who are suffering—and he also gave us the wonderful privilege of sharing with those in pain both the lessons of pain and also the solution to pain, Christ.

Let me also say that suffering was also designed for Christians.

We miss the whole meaning of the Christian faith when we live our lives seeking to avoid suffering and difficulty—trying to be comfortable physically, financially, emotionally, relationally, and spiritually. If this had been Jesus's goal, he would have stayed in heaven.

So many Christians seek to live the "pain-free" Christian life. Such a life has no impact. Discomfort and suffering are tools of God's discipleship in our lives, and thus part of the very good plan of God.

3. Not All Suffering Is the Same

Scripture reveals at least three types of suffering. One type is the suffering that is the consequence of our own sin. When you suffer like this, it's good to ask yourself a question that we often ask our children: "When does God love you?" The answer, thank God, is "All the time." We receive grace, love, and acceptance from the Father even in—especially in—times of suffering. But is suffering because of our own sin the bulk of our suffering?

Another type of suffering is what we could call "common suffering." This is suffering that affects people regardless of whether they are Christians or not—using the word *common* in a fashion similar to what we mean when we speak of "common grace." This is not suffering as a result of one's individual sin. It's just part of life in this fallen world. It includes health problems from colds to cancer. It includes hot weather, cold weather, earthquakes, and typhoons. It includes financial struggles and poverty. It includes suffering at the hands of others. It includes death itself. All people want to avoid this suffering, but we can't.

I'm thankful for the many people who prayed for my daughter Mikaela. We were so thankful to learn that her condition was not cancerous. She has yet to need surgery, but we continue to monitor her with regular MRIs. It has been a thorn for us to bear, but also an opportunity to testify of the sustaining grace and faithfulness of our Lord. The trust that Christians put in God in the midst of common suffering can be a tremendous witness to the gospel for those who don't know Christ.

Finally there is "Christ's suffering." This is suffering we experience because we are Christian, because we want to live for Jesus Christ. This includes suffering at home or work because of obeying Jesus; persecution from governments, companies, or even family members because of refusing to dishonor Christ; common suffering that is compounded because of following Christ—for example, suffering financially to help the poor or the lost, or to foster the spread of the gospel; and suffering poverty or danger by choice by living in deprived areas of the world so as to win people to the Lord Jesus.

Many Christians have rarely or never experienced such suffering. Our lives are so hidden, so innocuous to Satan's work, that they don't bother him at all.

How about you? What kinds of suffering do you endure? Suffering because of your own sin? "Common suffering" that is no different than that of non-Christians? Again, God is there for you in such suffering, and there is much of the gospel and grace to be known in such suffering. But do you know anything of what it means to suffer for Christ?

Now, of course, tabulating various kinds of suffering in some daily chart is not the point. The point is following Christ and accepting the very real, often difficult, always wonderful consequences of serving him.

Proclamation (vv. 22–31)

David learned these lessons, and the result was a completely changed life and attitude. In verses 22–31, we see a heart of trust and praise, and an exhortation to others to praise. We see in these verses the fruit of enduring suffering in faith, and that fruit is praise and proclamation.

First, in verse 22, we see individual praise: "I will tell of your name to my brothers; in the midst of the congregation I will praise you." This is the doxological instinct that is basic to the Christian life. It's why we sing!

In verse 23, we see David exhorting others to praise God, because it's not enough just for him to worship God:

> You who fear the LORD, praise him!
> All you offspring of Jacob, glorify him,
> and stand in awe of him, all you offspring of Israel!

Why do God's people praise him? Because he saves:

> For he has not despised or abhorred
> the affliction of the afflicted,
> and he has not hidden his face from him,
> but has heard, when he cried to him. (v. 24)

As we trust God and proclaim his faithfulness, we see that blessings flow. Both the poor (the "afflicted," v. 26) and the rich (the "prosperous," v. 29) are blessed: "The afflicted shall eat and be satisfied" (v. 26) and "All the prosperous of the earth eat and worship" (v. 29).

The Challenge of Psalm 22

Psalm 22:27 shows the extent of God's blessings and salvation: "All the ends of the earth shall remember and turn to the Lord, and all the families of the nations shall worship before you."

Here is a key lesson for the Christian. Yes, God is *my* God. However, the Christian response to the wonderful salvation of Christ should be: May *my* God be *their* God! Oh, may all the nations and all peoples worship Christ and be able to say to him, "My God." This is the missional instinct that should be basic to the Christian life.

Personal doxology is not enough—no Christian should be satisfied with personal worship alone when so many around the world have little or no opportunity even to hear the gospel, much less to worship the Lord of the universe.

Let me be clear here: worship is primary, not missions. But if the only purpose of God were our personal worship and our personal enjoyment of the gospel, then God would immediately sweep us up to heaven after we believe in him so that we could fulfill that sole purpose.

Why does God not do this? Because, in addition to our primary purpose of worship, we have been given a primary mission while on earth—the building of the kingdom of God, the hallowing of God's name by all of creation, and the worship of God by every tribe, language, people, and nation. That primary mission serves the primary purpose of worship. And that primary mission flows from that primary purpose. But that primary purpose is lost when that mission is neglected.

God's salvation for us personally is part of a big plan of salvation—from eternity past to eternity future, for every nation on earth. God invites us to be a part of that plan, to have a global doxological mission. David here is showing us how, by exhorting

Christians to worship God and also to call the world to join in that worship.

Psalm 22 and Jesus

Brothers and sisters, our suffering is not merely for our sanctification. It is to prepare us for proclamation of the difficulty of life in a fallen world, but also of the blessedness of God's grace that speaks into suffering, that sustains us through suffering, and that will ultimately rescue us from suffering.

In Psalm 22:30–31, we see the blessing of God on generation after generation. From suffering and the faithfulness of God, we see generational doxology of God—old, young, and future generations! In verse 31, we see generational *mission* as well—old, young, and future generations will testify and proclaim God's righteousness to all nations: "They shall come and proclaim his righteousness to a people yet unborn, that he has done it."

Worship now will become worship forever.

As we suffer and rely on God, testify of his faithfulness, and worship him, people are won to Christ. As evangelism and missions happen, we learn not just that God is faithful in our suffering or that he has purpose in it for us, but that suffering has a missional purpose with global implications.

Where there is the suffering of the godly, there is, in due time, the fruit of the gospel. Throughout the history of the church, we can see that God has worked his salvation through the suffering and testimonies of his people—individual by individual.

This is most true in the suffering of Jesus Christ. Jesus echoed the words of Psalm 22:1 on the cross. This psalm foreshadows his experience of suffering in our place for our sins. In these words, we see his suffering. He was surrounded by his enemies. They mocked him. He cried out to God.

David only *thought* that God had forsaken him. All Christians can have complete confidence that God will never leave us or forsake us. That is his promise. But God *did* turn his face from

Christ on the cross and poured out his wrath on the One who became a curse for us, in order that we might be delivered from death and saved eternally.

We question God: How could you allow me to suffer? How could you allow suffering even to exist if you are good?

Here is one of the amazing truths of Christianity: God not only allows, but *ordains* suffering. Why? Ultimately the greatest reason why suffering happens is so that Christ could suffer for us and display the most amazing love and sacrifice conceivable. Suffering exists because God ordained that Christ would suffer for sinners.

But it was a meaningful, purpose-filled suffering. And from that sacrifice, God will be glorified and worshiped by people throughout time and to the ends of the earth!

God worked his salvation through the suffering of Jesus Christ. How can we complain of our little suffering when we know how much Jesus suffered for us?

Don't run away from suffering. Not only is it a tool for your own discipleship in Jesus Christ, it is God's tool to bring salvation even to the ends of the earth.

Do we run toward suffering for the sake of suffering? Of course not. But we run toward Christ, and, as a consequence of following him, as he taught us, we have tribulation. There is a suffering that we will know, because all is not right in this world. But God has a plan for the redemption of his people, and that plan includes you.

And so, following Jesus to the cross, we take up our own crosses and experience the pain and joy of denying ourselves. Following him to the lost, we set aside social comfort, political correctness, and some of the freedoms of our own private space, time, and relational preferences. Following him in sacrifice, we deny ourselves financial comfort and pleasure so that others might have their daily bread and still others might come to know the Bread of Life.

And now, or perhaps in the future, following him even to the ends of the earth, we are willing to suffer the loss of family, friends, language, culture, and comfort that the worthy name of Jesus might be worshiped—that *our* God might become *their* God.

7

JESUS AND JUSTICE

Stephen Um

Every human being has an innate sense and a natural longing for justice. C. S. Lewis insightfully picks this up in his observations on how human beings argue with one another: "[People] say things like this: 'How'd you like it if anyone did the same to you?'—'That's my seat, I was there first'—'Leave him alone, he isn't doing you any harm.' . . . Quarrelling means trying to show that the other man is in the wrong. And there would be no sense in trying to do that unless you and he had some sort of agreement as to what Right and Wrong are."[1] Quarrelling is not just about trying to curb another person's behavioristic tendencies; it is about trying to make an argument that you are in the right and that the other individual is not.

About ten years ago, when my second daughter was around six years old, I was driving her to school, which was about twenty minutes away from our home. We were running a little late, and admittedly it was my fault because I had not planned accordingly. Just a few minutes into our ride, she started to get nervous. Eventually, she said, "Hey, Dad, can you get me there quickly?"

I responded, "I'll try my best."

---

[1] C. S. Lewis, *Mere Christianity* (New York: HarperCollins, 2001), 3–4.

She continued to grow more anxious and insecure, and then said again, "Daddy, hurry up; I can't be late!"

Attempting to ease her mind, I responded, "Honey, it's okay if we're a little bit late; what's the problem?"

She said, "Well, if I get three tardies, then I'm going to receive detention."

I thought: "Wow, what kind of school am I sending my daughter to? She's in kindergarten and she's going to get detention if she gets three tardies!" But I responded to her by saying, "Hey, I'll try my best."

Then, about thirty seconds later, she said: "Daddy, why should I get punished if it's your fault for getting me there late?" Her response showed that she had an innate sense for what was right and what was wrong. She knew that it would not be right for her to be punished for someone else's crime.

The issue of justice is complex. Michael Sandel, a political philosopher at Harvard, names three reigning paradigms for justice: maximizing welfare, respecting freedom, and promoting virtue.[2] The variety of perspectives on justice is also seen in the current American political spectrum, where views on justice have become polarized. On the right, there are those who say that justice is an individual, personal responsibility. On the left, there are those who say that it is a communal, state responsibility.

To make the matter more confusing, there are numerous Christian approaches to justice. On the one hand, some place all of their emphasis on the primacy of the declaration of the gospel—on preaching, disciple making, and evangelism. On the other hand, some place their entire emphasis on the demonstration of the gospel through deeds of justice and mercy.[3] The issue becomes even cloudier when we zoom in and ask, "What is the relationship between justice and the mission of the church?" Is the church's mission summed up, as many have argued, in the

---

[2] Michael J. Sandel, *Justice: What's the Right Thing to Do?* (New York: Farrar, Straus and Giroux, 2010), 6.
[3] These are simply the two poles on the spectrum. There are certainly many individuals who have found a more nuanced, balanced approach.

Great Commission—that the church is called primarily to evangelism, preaching, and disciple making? Or, as others have argued, does the mission of the church include cultural transformation and social reform? As you can see, the collision of the topics of justice and mission can create a perfect storm. The result is that Christians, churches, and theologians are regularly divided over this issue.

However, though there is confusion and controversy, we cannot shy away from talking about the issue of justice, for two reasons. First, practically speaking, there is simply too much injustice in the world for Christians not to say or do anything in response. Second, biblically speaking, there is just too much evidence that suggests that justice is very near to the heart of God.

Justice Defined

How should we define justice? Tim Keller offers one definition: "to 'do justice' means to go places where the fabric of shalom has broken down, where the weaker members of societies are falling through the fabric, and to repair it."[4] Implicit in this definition is a call to pursue justice whenever we find the world to be in a state in which it was not intended to be, and to seek out people who are in need and oppressed in order to relieve them of the burden. Justice is ordering the world according to the righteousness of God. God is just and righteous; he has created humanity in his image, and therefore we are called to reflect the image of God by doing justice.[5] To borrow another definition from Keller, doing justice is "giving humans their due as people in the image of God. We all agree that everyone deserves not to be enslaved, beaten, raped, or killed. We are not just talking about helping the poor but helping people whose rights are being violated."[6]

---

[4] Timothy Keller, *Generous Justice: How God's Grace Makes Us Just* (New York: Dutton, 2010), 177.
[5] Nicholas Wolterstorff, *Hearing the Call: Liturgy, Justice, Church, and World* (Grand Rapids: Eerdmans, 2011), 101.
[6] Timothy Keller, as interviewed by Kristen Scharold, "Tim Keller: What We Owe the Poor," christianity today.com, http://www.christianitytoday.com/ct/2010/december/10.69.html?paging=off.

Justice and the Character of God

Why is doing justice so bound up with the fact that human beings are made in the image of God? It is because the Bible grounds justice in the very character of God. Consider these passages:

> For the LORD your God is God of gods and Lord of lords, the great, the mighty, and the awesome God, who is not partial and takes no bribe. He executes justice for the fatherless and the widow, and loves the sojourner, giving him food and clothing. (Deut. 10:17–18)

> The Rock, his work is perfect, for all his ways are justice. A God of faithfulness and without iniquity, just and upright is he. (Deut. 32:4)

> I know that the LORD will maintain the cause of the afflicted, and will execute justice for the needy. (Ps. 140:12)

Similarly, we see that justice is to characterize God's covenant community. From the start, as they experienced the just character of God, his called-out people were to have an impulse to respond and re-image that character. And so they were commanded, "Learn to do good; seek justice, correct oppression; bring justice to the fatherless, plead the widow's cause" (Isa. 1:17), and, "Do not oppress the widow, the fatherless, the sojourner, or the poor, and let none of you devise evil against another in your heart" (Zech. 7:10). These verses provide a picture of what some have referred to as "the quartet of the vulnerable": the widow, the orphan, the immigrant, and the poor.[7] The Bible provides numerous structural provisions to ensure that the needs of these marginalized and needy individuals are met.

An example of this can be found in Leviticus 19:9–10. There, God commanded his people not to reap a field right up to its edge or to gather the fallen grapes in their vineyards. Why? The gleanings of the harvest and the fallen grapes were "for the poor and for the

---

[7] Nicholas Wolterstorff, *Justice: Rights and Wrongs* (Princeton, NJ: Princeton University Press, 2008), 76.

sojourner." Other examples of these structural provisions can be found in the Sabbath Year (Lev. 25:1–7) and the Year of Jubilee (Lev. 25:8ff.). These instructions were given to God's community to give them a means of responding to his just and righteous character by alleviating the burdens of the quartet of the vulnerable and others who were in need.

Of course, there are significant differences in how these verses are applied in our day and age, and we need to be careful in jumping too quickly from the context of the Old Testament covenant community to the present day. Kevin DeYoung and Greg Gilbert, in their book *What Is the Mission of the Church?*, have helpfully noted a few significant changes that we must keep in mind: we do not live in an ancient agrarian society; our property has not been directly assigned by God; our economy is not based on a fixed piece of land; and modern nations are not under the Mosaic covenant.[8] And yet, while there are clear changes in context and application, nothing has fundamentally changed when it comes to the character of God and how he understands justice. Similarly, there has been no change in the fact that the community of God's people has been called to reflect that character.

As we know, Jesus does not negate the Old Testament laws concerned with justice; rather, he consistently presses their application further. He calls for a righteousness exceeding that of the scribes and Pharisees (Matt. 5:20). And what was lacking in the righteousness of the scribes and Pharisees? Consider Matthew 23:23: "Woe to you, scribes and Pharisees, hypocrites! For you tithe mint and dill and cumin, and have neglected the weightier matters of the law: justice and mercy and faithfulness. These you ought to have done, without neglecting the others." Justice and mercy are "weightier matters."

These weightier matters are precisely what Jesus has in mind when he summarizes all the Old Testament law under the Great Commandment: "You shall love the Lord your God with all your

---

[8] Kevin DeYoung and Greg Gilbert, *What Is the Mission of the Church? Making Sense of Social Justice, Shalom, and the Great Commission* (Wheaton, IL: Crossway, 2011), 149–150.

heart and with all your soul and with all your mind. This is the great and first commandment. And a second is like it: You shall love your neighbor as yourself. On these two commandments depend all the Law and the Prophets" (Matt. 22:37–40). In essence, Jesus takes the Old Testament justice laws and claims that they are summed up in the New Testament understanding of "neighbor." From start to finish, then, the Bible gives us a consistent portrait of a God whose very character is one of justice and whose call upon his people is to reflect his justice to the world as they seek to love their neighbors in the way that he loves them.

The Character of Biblical Justice

Throughout all of Scripture, justice is seen to be *grace fueled*. Consider Deuteronomy 10:18–19: "He executes justice for the fatherless and the widow, and loves the sojourner, giving him food and clothing. *Love the sojourner, therefore, for you were sojourners in the land of Egypt.*" Again we see that justice is a part of God's character, but on what basis are his people directed to reflect this just character? They are to understand their just actions as arising from their rescue and redemption from Egypt: "Love the sojourner . . . [because] you were sojourners." It is as if God were saying, "Because I have delivered you—because I rescued you when you were living as aliens in Egypt—you ought to have a burden to deliver those who are in need." The call to justice is rooted in the deliverance and salvation that God has provided for his people. It is grace fueled. Keller gets at this grace-fueled dynamic better than anyone: "Those who are middle-class in spirit tend to be indifferent to the poor, but people who come to grasp the gospel of grace and become spiritually poor find their hearts gravitating toward the materially poor."[9] The recognition of God's grace to us in our spiritual poverty leads to our pursuit of justice for those experiencing material poverty. When the gospel grabs our hearts, we are moved to pursue justice.

Biblical justice is also *holistic*. To observe Jesus's ministry is to

---

[9] Keller, *Generous Justice*, 102.

see him meeting not only spiritual needs, but also the physical, material, and psychological needs of individuals whom he encounters. Jesus heals the physically broken, feeds the hungry, exorcises demons from the oppressed, cares for social outcasts, provides dignity for the undignified, and offers consolation to those who mourn. Biblical justice, as it is on display in the life of Jesus, is trenchantly holistic. Although there is reason to recognize the primacy of spiritual salvation and mercy (see Mark 2:10), we do not have warrant to emphasize that spiritual work to the exclusion of material justice. Jesus's life, ministry, death, and resurrection demonstrate that his work of reconciliation has very real implications for the physical world in which we live.

An honest reading of the Bible's perspective on justice must also come to terms with its *radical* nature. The justice that Jesus calls for is one that demands his followers' total allegiance. The radical nature of the gospel essentially reorders the "give-to-get" economy with which we are so familiar. Consider Luke 14:13–14: "But when you give a feast, invite the poor, the crippled, the lame, the blind, and you will be blessed, because they cannot repay you." Note that, in context, Jesus is primarily concerned not with giving guidelines for how to throw a party, but with challenging the give-to-get economy under which the Pharisees are operating. They throw parties and invite honorable guests in order to be invited to parties thrown by honorable hosts. Jesus is suggesting that they radically flip this on its head. He is making the point that, if you know the unrepayable, nonmercenary nature of God's grace, it is borne out in your actions: you engage in one-way giving, being radically generous with your time, money, and relational capital. In other words, those who have received a gift that they can never repay are those who have the resources to give away gifts that can never be repaid.

Now, almost as soon as we start to grasp the radical nature of biblical justice, we find our inner Pharisees speaking up: "There has to be a limit to this! How far-reaching must this justice be before enough is enough?" Biblically speaking, however, the scope of justice is *universal*. Jesus addresses the pharisaic impulse to put achievable limits on the radical call to justice in the parable of the good Samaritan. In that classic text, Jesus expands the biblical concept of "neighbor" to mean something beyond our families, friends, and next-door neighbors. He even extends "neighbor" beyond our local churches and those who share our faith. Self-giving, one-way, justice-based love is to be given to all who are in need, even (and especially) our "enemies." The scope of biblical justice is shockingly and scandalously universal.

Finally, biblical justice is *eternally significant*. While we must be careful not to imply that acts of justice are the grounds for a right relationship with God, Jesus's discussion of justice in the context of final judgment implies that a life of justice is evidence of that right relationship (Matt. 25:31–46). Justice is not an accessory—something that we optionally add to the Christian life to make it more attractive. It is a necessity. If we have received the grace of God declared to us in the gospel, it follows that we demonstrate the upside-down dynamic of the gospel in the way we handle issues of justice and mercy.

The character of biblical justice is robust and thoroughgoing. It is not coerced by the force of law but compelled by the fuel of grace. It does not approach humans as piecemeal creatures but as whole people in need of holistic justice. It turns the give-to-get economy of this world on its head in favor of a radical, nonmercenary, self-giving love. It refuses pharisaic attempts at limitation, instead pressing us to understand the universal character of "neighbor." And, rather than being a temporary accessory, biblical justice is seen to be a permanent necessity with eternal significance.

Justice Denied

The trouble with a definition like the one above is that it quickly and effectively puts biblical justice out of our reach. Evidence suggests that rather than carrying out the kind of justice called for in Scripture, human beings have a tendency to deny justice with their actions (or lack of action). Let us consider three ways that we are prone to deny justice.

Denial #1: Valuing the External over the Internal

We deny justice when we hypocritically or legalistically value the external over the internal—when we are more concerned with outside appearances than inward realities. This is precisely what Jesus is driving at when he speaks of two trees: one bearing good fruit, the other bearing bad fruit (Matt. 7:15–20). Note that Jesus is not contrasting someone who does good deeds with someone who does not. Both trees are bearing fruit; on the outside, they appear to be very similar. Instead, Jesus is contrasting a gospel-fueled individual who produces healthy fruit (which results from the tree's internal soundness) with a religious individual who produces diseased fruit (which results from the tree's internal rottenness).

When you compare a pharisaical religious person with a grace-fueled Christian, the external "fruit" of both individuals may look quite similar. They both read the Scriptures. They both evangelize. They both strive toward obedience. They both tithe. They both do "justice." And the Pharisee may even do all of this more rigidly and consistently than does the Christian. What, then, is the deciding factor between healthy, sumptuous fruit and diseased, rotten fruit? In short, it is a question of internal heart motivation. The hypocrites are those who are eager to receive praise from others for their apparent righteousness and extravagant good deeds (e.g. "doing justice"). When they give to the needy, they sound trumpets in the streets so as to be noticed (Matt. 6:2). Grace-fueled justice, on the other hand, works without regard for acclaim or praise, and has the glory of God as its ultimate aim.

Consider Jesus's rather direct words to the Pharisees in Matthew 23:27–28: "Woe to you, scribes and Pharisees, hypocrites! For you are like whitewashed tombs, which outwardly appear beautiful, but within are full of dead people's bones and all uncleanness. So you also outwardly appear righteous to others, but within you are full of hypocrisy and lawlessness." Here Jesus expresses the primacy of the internal heart motive over the external display. He is not suggesting that we ought not to engage in acts that "appear righteous." Rather, he is saying that external appearance is not a sufficient motivation for biblical justice and righteousness.

Valuing the external over internal motivation guarantees the denial of justice. If the external is your primary motivation, you do justice only when someone is watching and there is something to be gained. You continue to overlook the overlooked because you have no motivation to do justice when no one is looking. You continue to marginalize the marginalized because there is nothing to drive you to the margins if you are set on being the center of attention. Only the resources of the gospel can overcome the denial of justice that results when the external is valued over the internal.

Denial #2: Aiming for the Measurable over the Radical

Because of the innate human desire to justify ourselves—to prove that we are right and valuable—we deny justice by reducing its radical nature to something measurable. We are dying to believe that we can obey, and so we reduce and redefine the demands of radical justice until nothing radical remains. We see this dynamic at work in the Sermon on the Mount. Jesus is interacting with the laws of the Old Testament and the religious traditions that have been built up around them. He says, "You have heard that it was said, 'You shall love your neighbor and hate your enemy'" (Matt. 5:43). Any faithful reader of the Old Testament Scriptures is familiar with the command to "love your neighbor as yourself" (Lev. 19:18), but in that command we find no mention of hating one's enemy. In fact, we see just the opposite: a command not to bear a grudge or take vengeance. This gives us insight into what Jesus means when he says, "You have heard that it was said." He is pointing not primarily to Leviticus, but to the traditional Jewish interpretation of this law, which had appended the phrase, "and hate your enemy."

Now, the natural question is, "Why would anyone want to add

to the law of God?" Don't we have enough laws in the Old Testament? Why is it that there are large books of commentary—such as the Mishnah, the Talmud, and the Targum—that explain the law and how we ought to go about observing it? In short, the reason all of this was added to the law—the reason the Jewish tradition appended the phrase "and hate your enemy" to the command to "love your neighbor"—is that it made obedience to the radical command measurable. The undoable command became doable. And once the law is obeyable, it appears that self-justification is within reach. "Hey, I'm loving my neighbor and I'm hating my enemies!" Everyone I love is conveniently placed under the category of "neighbor," and everyone I hate is simply an "enemy." The result is the nullification of the radical demand of the law. It now has little to no effect on my life. I have simply reinterpreted it so that it is in accord with the way I am already living my life—loving some people and hating others! When you make the demand of radical justice measurable, you miss the very reason for which the law was given. We are meant to gaze into the radical, immeasurable mirror of the law and find ourselves utterly lacking, unable to measure up, and in need of a Savior. The radical demand of justice was never meant to be the means of our salvation, but rather the means of pointing us to a Savior.

Furthermore, if justice ceases to be radical and is made measurable—if it is simply done out of self-interest—it ceases to be justice. If the goal is measurement for the sake of self-justification, we are only ever as just as we need to be in order to satisfy ourselves. We do justice not for the one in need, but for ourselves. And we do justice only to the extent that it satisfies our desires, with little regard for the actual needs of our neighbors. Aiming for the measurable over the radical is a surefire path to the denial of biblical justice.

Denial #3: Settling for the Limited over the Universal
Ultimately, to move from the radical to the measurable is to reframe the character of biblical justice. And once we redefine what

it means to be "just," we consistently settle for the limited over the universal. We can be content when our limited, self-centered needs are met, leaving us without the resources to address the far-reaching needs of others. So the move from universal to limited is a result of self-absorption. When we are narcissistically self-absorbed, our love for ourselves trumps our love for others. In contrast, the gospel calls us to reverse this order, putting the needs of others before our own. Ed Welch says: "Regarding other people, our problem is that we *need* them (for ourselves) more than we *love* them (for the glory of God). The task God sets for us is to need them *less* and love them *more*."[10]

When we are self-centered and consumed with our own needs, we are, in turn, needy, controlling, and emotionally deficient. We do not have the necessary emotional capital to do justice, to show mercy, and to walk humbly with God (Mic. 6:8). Galatians 5:26 refers to this when it challenges us not to be "vainglorious, provoking one another, envying one another" (ASV). "Vainglorious" is a good translation of the Greek word, which might more literally be translated as "empty-glory." This is to say that when we are empty of glory—when there is a glory vacuum within us—the natural tendency is to view others as manipulable objects that must be acted upon to fill us up and to give us meaning. What happens when there is a glory vacuum in our hearts?[11] We provoke those who are below us and we envy those who are above us. We are only as generous as we want to be with as few people as possible, and we feel justified in doing so. Needless to say, in order for us to pursue the universal implications of biblical justice, our self-absorption needs to be overcome—our glory vacuum has to be filled with a true glory.

The question is, "How?" How can our consistent denial of justice be overcome? Where can we find the resources to overcome

---

[10] Edward T. Welch, *When People Are Big and God Is Small: Overcoming Peer Pressure, Codependency, and the Fear of Man* (Phillipsburg, NJ: P&R, 1997), 19.

[11] I'm indebted to Tim Keller for the language of "glory vacuum." See Timothy Keller, *Galatians For You* (Epsom, Surrey, England: The Good Book Company, 2013), 164.

our tendency to value the external, to aim at the measurable, and to settle for the limited? How can we pursue a biblical justice that is internally grace fueled, radical in character, and universal in its scope?

Justice Delivered

You may have heard the basic distinction between grace and mercy described in this way:

> Mercy is not getting what we deserve.
> Grace is getting what we do not deserve.[12]

When we attempt to summarize biblical justice in a similar (admittedly truncated) fashion, we arrive at the following:

> Justice is getting what we do deserve, either for protection or punishment.

That is to say, justice is a double-edged sword. Justice protects the oppressed and punishes the guilty. The trouble is that every human being is *both* oppressed *and* guilty. By virtue of being made in God's image, and as a result of God's common grace, every human being deserves the justice of protection from oppression. The vulnerable, the marginalized, the needy—all of these individuals have a right to receive protective justice.[13] However, by virtue of our sin and guilt before God, every human being also deserves the justice of punishment for transgression. We are guilty before a holy God, who holds us accountable for our sins.

How, then, do those who deserve the punishment of justice come to the point where they can be purveyors and agents of protective justice? How do those who have so consistently denied justice become those who seek to be deliverers of protective justice? The

---

[12] The original source of this popular summary is unclear. For one example, see Charles R. Wood, *Sermon Outlines for Expository Preaching* (Grand Rapids: Kregel, 1998), 35.

[13] Furthermore, even though we may not view ourselves as members of the quartet of the marginalized, each of us, in varying degrees, experiences need and is under the "oppression" of idols and/or ungodly structures that bend toward injustice. All human beings, regardless of their perception of their current standing, are entitled to protective justice by virtue of having been created in the image of God.

answer is that we need One who is able to absorb the punishing, penal justice on our behalf. We need One who is willing to forgo his right to protective justice in order to receive the penalty of punishing justice in our place. And this is precisely what we have in Christ Jesus: One who was willingly denied protective justice in order to deliver those who are under the bondage of slavery to sin. This radical work of justice has profound implications for the way we approach issues of justice today. We'll consider just two of them.

First, when we realize that Christ graciously absorbed the punishing justice of God to secure us a protected status in the presence of God, our motivation for doing justice shifts. Namely, we begin to be fueled by grace. No longer is justice motivated by external demand (which is limited in its ability to produce heart change); instead, it is motivated by internal heart transformation. No longer do we do justice to earn right standing in the eyes of God, others, or even ourselves; instead, we do justice for justice's sake, because we have been given right standing in the eyes of God.

Grace-fueled justice is grounded in the justifying work of Jesus. Consider Christ's justifying work as it is expounded in 1 John 1:9: "If we confess our sins, he is faithful and just to forgive us our sins and to cleanse us from all unrighteousness." A handful of commentators have noted what this text does *not* say: "If we confess our sins, he is faithful and *merciful* . . ."[14] What is the importance of God's just nature in this context? Why does the text say that he is faithful and *just*? It does so because when we confess our sins before the tribunal of God's holiness and judgment, we are effectively and ultimately pleading for justice. If Jesus died on the cross for us—paid the price for our sins, received the penal judgment we deserved—then God's forgiveness is synonymous with his justice! The payment has already been made; the punishment has already been received. When we confess our sins, God is *just* in forgiving us because of the work of Christ. He never asks us to pay for our sins because he has provided payment for us in Jesus.

---

[14] Timothy Keller, "Jesus Our Defense—1," sermon preached at Redeemer Presbyterian Church, New York, NY, October 23, 1994.

God doesn't double dip.[15] He is just. When we receive this kind of radical, consistent, justifying grace, we can't help but respond with grace-fueled justice that seeks to meet the needs of our neighbors. We can be gracious because we have received grace. We can be merciful because we have been shown mercy. And we can be radically generous in doing justice because God was radically generous in the way he justly justified us!

Second, the scope of our radically just response to the crying needs in our world is dramatically expanded. The gospel explodes and expands our understanding of "neighbor." We get a glimpse of this broadening scope of radical justice in 2 Samuel 9. There we encounter a man by the name of Mephibosheth. He was the son of Jonathan and the grandson of Saul. Samuel recounts that during the time of David's ascension to the throne, some sort of accident occurred in which a young Mephibosheth became physically disabled (2 Sam. 4:4). Given all that had transpired between his grandfather Saul and David, and in the wake of his father Jonathan's death, Mephibosheth had at some point decided to live in a remote place called Lo-debar, which likely means "no pasture" or "no word." Essentially, he was seeking refuge, and in order to find it, he had to live outside of the covenant community of God's people in an isolated place.

Eventually, something incredible occurs in the heart of King David, which can be understood only as the radical grace of God at work. David asks, "Is there still anyone left of the house of Saul, that I may show him kindness for Jonathan's sake?" (2 Sam. 9:1). Consider the nature of this question. He is essentially saying: "Are any of my enemy's descendants remaining? I want to show them kindness!" This is counterintuitive to say the least. A former servant of Saul named Ziba answers David: yes, Mephibosheth is the one remaining member of the house of Saul. Having found this out, David sends for him.

---

[15] In the words of John Owen, "A second payment of a debt once paid, or a requiring of it, is not answerable to the justice which God demonstrated in setting forth Christ to be a propitiation for our sins, Rom. iii. 25." (*The Death of Death in the Death of Christ* [Carlisle, PA: Banner of Truth, 2002], 161).

Now imagine the situation from Mephibosheth's perspective. He is physically disabled, and he has sought shelter in a veritable no man's land. Though life is difficult, he is living in a relatively peaceful state. But then he hears the knock on his door that he never wanted to hear. The king wants to see him. He must feel as though judgment day has come. In short order, Mephibosheth is brought before the king, and he does the only thing he knows to do: he prostrates himself. He knows that David has every right to do away with him—to have him wiped out because of his relationship to the house of Saul. So he bows before the king, demonstrating his utter neediness and helplessness.

What does David do? In a radical demonstration of grace that must come as a total shock to Mephibosheth, David responds with kindness: "And David said to him, 'Do not fear, for I will show you kindness for the sake of your father Jonathan, and I will restore to you all the land of Saul your father, and you shall eat at my table always'" (2 Sam. 9:7). David welcomes Mephibosheth into his court to be treated as though he were a son of the king. Furthermore, he gives all of Saul's land to Mephibosheth, and instructs Ziba that he and his household will now be Mephibosheth's servants. And how does Mephibosheth respond to this remarkable news? His reply is one of stunned gratitude: "What is your servant, that you should show regard for a dead dog such as I?" (v. 8). Grace has taken a grandson of the enemy, a self-proclaimed "dead dog," and made him an adopted child of the king (v. 11).

You can imagine what this would have done in the heart of Mephibosheth. Now, do you think that Mephibosheth doubted at times? Of course he did! There were times when he looked around the king's court and thought, "I don't belong here." As he looked at all the children of David, he had to have wondered what he was doing there. But every time he doubted, where would he look? Where would he find his hope? He found it in the gospel according to David, which was, "I will show you kindness on account of another."

Later in 2 Samuel, an interesting twist is added to the story. Ziba, the man charged with caring for Mephibosheth and his land, decides that he has had enough of serving the grandson of his former master Saul. He devises a plan to make the king believe that Mephibosheth is a traitor who has little care for David's well-being and honor. At first, David is taken in by Ziba's lies, but eventually the truth is brought to light. Here's the scene: David is returning to Jerusalem, and he has been led to believe that Mephibosheth is a backstabber. To his surprise, when he returns to Jerusalem, Mephibosheth is there to greet him. Observe Mephibosheth to see the way that grace transforms an individual's heart and devotion:

> And Mephibosheth the son of Saul came down to meet the king. He had neither taken care of his feet nor trimmed his beard nor washed his clothes, from the day the king departed until the day he came back in safety. And when he came to Jerusalem to meet the king, the king said to him, "Why did you not go with me, Mephibosheth?" He answered, "My lord, O king, my servant deceived me, for your servant said to him, 'I will saddle a donkey for myself, that I may ride on it and go with the king.' For your servant is lame. He has slandered your servant to my lord the king. But my lord the king is like the angel of God; do therefore what seems good to you. For all my father's house were but men doomed to death before my lord the king, but you set your servant among those who eat at your table. What further right have I, then, to cry to the king?" And the king said to him, "Why speak any more of your affairs? I have decided: you and Ziba shall divide the land." And Mephibosheth said to the king, "Oh, let him take it all, since my lord the king has come safely home." (2 Sam. 19:24–30)

Listen to his heart. This is someone who understands the life-transforming, internal heart dynamics of grace. He understands that God desires a radical interior radiance, not just hypocritical external activity. He understands that, on account of another, he received mercy rather than judgment, and it has stirred and moved him to the point where his central concern is the well-being of the king. Rather than having a sense of entitlement, he recognizes that he has received that to which he is not entitled. If he had gotten what he deserved, he would have experienced death and judgment. Instead, he has received what he did not deserve, namely, the undeserved favor of the king.

Amazingly, we have been shown an even greater grace than that which was shown to Mephibosheth. We have something more than the gospel according to David. We have been given the gospel of Jesus, which says that we have received mercy on account of another who is greater than Jonathan. Jesus Christ absorbed the penal justice of God in order that we might receive the mercy of God. And the result is that our hearts are stirred to have a willingness to suffer and to be disadvantaged for those who are in desperate need. In Christ, the ultimately strong, rich person disadvantaged himself for the weak and the poor, in order that we who are poor and weak might become rich and strong in him. In light of this startling grace, we are called to live a life that demonstrates the generous, just, merciful, and sacrificial self-giving of God. Because of Jesus's self-donation, we have the emotional and spiritual capital to do just that.

CONTRIBUTORS

D. A. Carson

D. A. Carson (PhD, University of Cambridge) is cofounder and president of The Gospel Coalition and since 1978 has taught at Trinity Evangelical Divinity School (Deerfield, IL), where he currently serves as Research Professor of New Testament. He came to Trinity from Northwest Baptist Theological Seminary in Vancouver, British Columbia, and has served in pastoral ministry in Canada and the United Kingdom. He and his wife, Joy, have two children.

Andrew Davis

Andrew Davis is senior pastor of the First Baptist Church, Durham, North Carolina. He studied at Massachusetts Institute of Technology, Gordon-Conwell Theological Seminary (MDiv), and the Southern Baptist Theological Seminary (PhD). He has also worked as a mechanical engineer in Massachusetts and church planted in Tokushima, Japan, through the Southern Baptist Convention's International Mission Board. He and his wife, Christi, have five children.

Michael Oh

Michael Oh is the executive director/CEO of The Lausanne Movement. He is the founder and board chair of CBI Japan in Nagoya, Japan, which includes Christ Bible Seminary, church-planting efforts, and outreach ministries. He studied Harvard University (MA); Trinity Evangelical Divinity School (MDiv); and the University of Pennsylvania (PhD, MS). Michael and his wife, Pearl, have five children.

John Piper

John Piper is founder and teacher of Desiring God (DesiringGod. org), chancellor of Bethlehem College and Seminary, and a founding council member of The Gospel Coalition. For thirty-three years he served as senior pastor at Bethlehem Baptist Church (Minneapolis). He studied at Wheaton College; Fuller Theological Seminary (BD); and the University of Munich (DTh). He and his wife, Noel, have four sons, one daughter, and a growing number of grandchildren.

David Platt

David Platt is president of the Southern Baptist Convention's International Mission Board and former senior pastor of The Church at Brook Hills in Birmingham, Alabama. He studied at the University of Georgia (BA, ABJ) and the New Orleans Baptist Theological Seminary (MDiv, ThM, PhD). He served at the New Orleans Baptist Theological Seminary as dean of chapel and assistant professor of expository preaching and apologetics, and as staff evangelist at Edgewater Baptist Church in New Orleans. He is the founder of Radical (Radical.net), a resource ministry dedicated to serving the church in making disciples of all nations. David and his wife, Heather, have four children.

J. Mack Stiles

J. Mack Stiles is CEO of Gulf Digital Solutions and general secretary for the Fellowship of Christian UAE Students (FOCUS) in the United Arab Emirates. He lives in Dubai with his wife, Leeann, and has worked for many years with InterVarsity Christian Fellowship in the United States. Mack is an elder at Redeemer Church of Dubai.

Stephen Um

Stephen Um (PhD, University of St. Andrews) is senior pastor of Citylife Presbyterian Church of Boston. He also teaches New Testament at Gordon-Conwell Theological Seminary and serves as associate training director with Redeemer City to City. Stephen and his wife, Kathleen, have been involved in several Presbyterian churches throughout the northeastern United States.

GENERAL INDEX

general revelation, 85, 92
Gilbert, Greg, 119
glory vacuum, 126
God: character of and justice, 118–20; sovereignty of, 106, 96–101
gospel, the: belief in and proclamation of, 30–36; as displaying the glory of Christ, 18–21; as good news, 20; the gospel theme as starting in Genesis and continuing throughout Scripture, 76; as the measure of all of life, 72
gospel ministry: as characterized by paradoxical death to self and overflowing life in Christ, 21–25; for the sake of God's glory, 38–41; for the sake of people, 36–38; and integrity, 13–18. *See also* new covenant, ministry of
Great Commandment, 119–20
Great Commission, 11, 30, 41, 46, 117; in John, 93; in Luke, 93; in Mark, 92–93; in Matthew, 92

Hart, Joseph, 88
Heart & Soul Café, 109
Heyerdahl, Thor, 98
Hilderbrand, Haley, 105
Hinduism, 40, 82
Holy Spirit, 11; as a down payment, 53; and missions, 29, 99
hyperbolen (Greek: beyond all measure and proportion), 46

image of God, 67; Jesus as the image of God, 19; and justice, 117, 118
inclusivism, 82
India, 31, 40; Bihar, 36–38; North India, 31–32
infants who die, 97n12
integrity, 13–18
International Mission Board, 49
Isaac, 76
Islam, 41, 69, 82

Jacob, 10; twelve sons of, 10
Japan, 40, 107–8; Nagoya, 108
Jesus, 11; cross work of, 20; as the fulfillment of the Old Testament sacrificial system (the Lamb of God), 75, 87; glory of, 18–21; as the Good Shepherd, 11; great events in his mission, 12; as the High Priest, 11; as the image of God, 19; as the Judge of all the earth, 58, 59, 97n11; as the King, 11; as the Lion of the tribe of Judah, 10; as Lord, 19–20, 40; love of as motivating the sharing of our faith, 65–66; ministry of, 120–21; on "neighbor," 120, 122, 124–25; obedience of, 11–12; and the Old Testament law, 119–20; as a propitiation, 90; and Psalm 22, 112–13; resurrection of, 32–33; shed blood

of as the only way for sinners to be saved, 86–89; as the Word of God, 11
Judges, book of, 10
judgment day, 58, 59, 97nn11–12
Judson, Adoniram, 52–53
justice: and the character of God, 118–20; Christian approaches to, 116; definition of, 117; perspectives on justice in the current American political spectrum, 116, 116n3; and the "quartet of the vulnerable," 118; three reigning paradigms for (maximizing welfare, respecting freedom, and promoting virtue), 116. *See also* justice, biblical, character of; justice, delivery of; justice, denial of
justice, biblical character of: as eternally significant, 122; as grace-fueled, 120; as holistic, 120–21; as radical in nature, 121–22; as universal in scope, 121–22
justice, delivery of: and the expansion of our understanding of "neighbor," 129–32; and Jesus's absorbing the punishing, penal justice on our behalf, 128; and our being fueled by grace, 128–29; the recipients of protective justice, 127, 127n13
justice, denial of: by aiming for the measurable over the radical, 124–25; by settling for the limited over the universal, 125–28; by valuing the external over the internal, 123–24

Keller, Timothy, 117, 120, 126n11, 128

Laos, 40
Lewis, C. S., 67, 115
Lindbeck, George, 83n5

MacArthur, John, 77, 84
Mecca, 41
Melchizedek, 82, 90
Mephibosheth, 129–32
Middle East, 35, 41
Mishnah, 125
missions, 49; frontier missions, 49; goal of (to make disciples of all peoples), 29; the heart of biblical missions, 25; and the Holy Spirit, 29, 99; local evangelism, 49. *See also* missions, courage in
missions case studies: Akil and Nisin, 73–74; Anil and Hari, 37–38; Linda, 68; Mohammed, 77–78; Nastaran, 69–70; Yuna, 70
missions, courage in, 51; and realism, 52–53; and resurrection, 54–56; and reunion, 56–57; and reward, 57–59
Moses, 13
Murray, John, 89

Nepal, 40
new covenant, ministry of, 13–14, 20
new creation, 68–69

SCRIPTURE INDEX

THE GOSPEL **COALITION**

The Gospel Coalition is a fellowship of evangelical churches deeply committed to renewing our faith in the gospel of Christ and to reforming our ministry practices to conform fully to the Scriptures. We have committed ourselves to invigorating churches with new hope and compelling joy based on the promises received by grace alone through faith alone in Christ alone.

We desire to champion the gospel with clarity, compassion, courage, and joy—gladly linking hearts with fellow believers across denominational, ethnic, and class lines. We yearn to work with all who, in addition to embracing our confession and theological vision for ministry, seek the lordship of Christ over the whole of life with unabashed hope in the power of the Holy Spirit to transform individuals, communities, and cultures.

Join the cause and visit TGC.org for fresh resources that will equip you to love God with all your heart, soul, mind, and strength, and to love your neighbor as yourself.

TGC.org

Also Available from
The Gospel Coalition